MICROWAVE
COOKBOOK

SAMSUNG

To Our Valued Customer:

Welcome to one of the most versatile cooking appliances ever invented! Your new microwave oven can help you prepare nutritious meals so quickly and conveniently, you'll wonder how you ever cooked without it.

At SAMSUNG, we believe that our technology and consumer products can help make your life easier. Use this cookbook as your "road map" to better, faster cooking with your new microwave oven. Be sure to read the oven use and care manual and the introduction to this cookbook so you learn how to get the most from microwave cooking. We're sure that this new SAMSUNG microwave oven will quickly become your favorite appliance, providing many satisfying cooking experiences.

PRECAUTIONS TO AVOID POSSIBLE EXPOSURE TO EXCESSIVE MICROWAVE ENERGY

(a) Do not attempt to operate this oven with the door open since open-door operation can result in harmful exposure to microwave energy. It is important not to defeat or tamper with the safety interlocks.

(b) Do not place any object between the oven front face and the door or allow soil or cleaner residue to accumulate on sealing surfaces.

(c) Do not operate the oven if it is damaged. It is particularly important that the oven door close properly and that there is no damage to the:
  (1) door (bent)
  (2) hinges and latches (broken or loosened)
  (3) door seals and sealing surfaces

(d) The oven should not be adjusted or repaired by anyone except properly qualified service personnel.

CONTENTS

INTRODUCING MICROWAVING   4

APPETIZERS   22

SOUPS, SANDWICHES & BEVERAGES   30

BEEF   44

PORK   62

LAMB   74

POULTRY   80

FISH & SEAFOOD   92

EGGS & CHEESE   100

SAUCES   106

VEGETABLES   110

PASTAS, CEREALS & GRAINS   120

BREADS   126

DESSERTS   132

SPECIAL IDEAS   148

INTRODUCING
MICROWAVING

HOW MICROWAVES COOK

Like radio waves only much shorter in length, the microwaves generated by your microwave oven are high frequency electromagnetic waves. Food in the oven absorbs microwaves, causing the food molecules to vibrate. The vibration causes friction which produces heat in the areas of penetration. Cooking begins in these areas and spreads by conduction to other parts of the food.

One common misconception about microwaves is that they cook food from the inside out. Actually, microwaves penetrate food from the outside to a depth of about one inch. Microwaves penetrate from all directions, so small foods are penetrated to the center from all sides.

Microwaves pass through materials such as glass, ceramics, paper and plastics. Containers made of these materials are ideal for microwave cooking because they allow microwaves to pass through and be absorbed by the food.

Microwaves are reflected by metal. Metal pans or dishes with metal trim are not suitable for microwave cooking because they reflect microwave energy away from the food. Aluminum foil can be used in small amounts to shield areas of food from overcooking, since foil also reflects microwaves.

Microwaves are absorbed by food or other moist objects in the microwave oven. Friction from the vibration of the molecules causes the food to cook. Heat travels from the outside to the center of large foods by conduction.

MICROWAVE UTENSILS

Containers which allow microwaves to pass through are suitable for microwave cooking. You probably already have several microwave-safe utensils. Many types of glass, stoneware, porcelain, pottery, china and glass ceramic (such as Corning Ware®) are good choices. To be suitable for microwaving, these dishes must not have metallic trim or glazes containing metal. If you are not sure a container is microwave-safe, test it using the technique described on the following page. Boilable pouches and oven cooking bags are ideal for microwaving (see page 9 for proper closures for oven cooking bags). Most paper containers and plastics that are not labeled microwave-safe are not recommended for microwave cooking. They may melt or distort during prolonged contact with very hot food.

Many utensils made especially for microwaving are now available. These are made of special plastics, many of which can withstand high temperatures (up to 400°F) in both microwave and conventional ovens. These utensils can go directly from freezer to microwave without breaking. Some, such as round muffin pans and ring baking dishes, are designed to arrange foods for even exposure to microwave energy. Microwave roasting racks elevate meat so it doesn't steam in its own juices. Many racks are designed to fit in a standard oblong baking dish.

UTENSILS, continued

Do not use metal pans or dishes with metallic trim, handles or screws. Metal reflects microwave energy and prevents it from reaching and cooking the food. Also unsuitable for use in the microwave oven are paper-covered metal twist-ties, foil-lined packages, pottery with a metal glaze, conventional meat or candy thermometers, and some types of dinnerware such as Centura® or Melamine®. Use aluminum foil to shield areas from overcooking (see page 12), but be sure to keep foil at least 1 inch away from the oven walls. Shallow foil trays, such as those used to package frozen dinners, can be used with the covering removed. Heating will occur as microwaves penetrate the food through the exposed top surface.

Test a dish if you are not sure that it is microwave-safe. Measure 1 cup water in a glass measure. Place on or beside the dish you are testing. Microwave at HIGH for 1 to 2 minutes, or until water is hot. If the dish remains cool, it is safe to use in the microwave oven.

Create your own microwave utensils by combining ones you already have. Place a drinking glass, right side up, in a 2-quart round casserole to make a ring-shaped dish for cakes or meatloaves. Use a saucer instead of a roasting rack to elevate meat in an oblong baking dish.

Depth of containers affects the cooking time. Food in a shallow casserole will microwave more quickly than food in a deep casserole with the same capacity. Cooking time is shortened because a greater surface area of food is exposed to microwave energy. Choose straight-sided dishes, since these keep the depth of food uniform so it cooks more evenly.

Shape of containers affects how evenly foods cook. Foods in round dishes cook more evenly than foods in square or rectangular dishes, since the latter allow microwaves to penetrate the corners from both sides, often resulting in overcooking. Ring shapes allow microwaves to penetrate from the center as well as the sides, for faster and more even cooking.

COVERINGS

Glass cover is used for steaming foods. It holds in steam when microwaving foods like vegetables which require little added moisture. A microwave-safe plate can substitute for a glass cover.

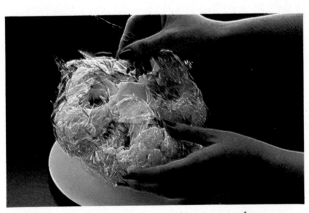

Plastic wrap forms a convenient cover for steaming. Fold back one edge slightly to form a vent to prevent the wrap from splitting. Wrap large whole foods like cauliflower in plastic wrap and steam them without using a dish, if desired.

Wax paper is a loose covering that prevents spatters and holds in heat to speed cooking. Cover foods with wax paper when you desire a moist but not steamed result.

Glass cover with wax paper makes a tighter seal when the cover is loose-fitting. Place a sheet of wax paper between the dish and the lid to retain more steam and reduce evaporation.

Oven cooking bags are ideal for microwaving less-tender cuts of meat or poultry. Tie the bag loosely with a string, nylon closure or piece of plastic cut from the bag (**not** a metal twist-tie) so some steam can escape.

Paper towels prevent spatters and retain some steam. They also absorb excess moisture from the surface of breads during reheating. Recycled paper is not recommended for use in the microwave oven.

MICROWAVING COOKING PRINCIPLES

Characteristics of foods determine how fast and evenly they cook in the microwave oven. Foods high in sugar, fat or water cook faster since these ingredients attract more microwave energy than other kinds of food molecules. Some of the other principles illustrated here are unique to microwaving; some are common to both microwave and conventional cooking. Study them to better understand how different kinds of food react during microwaving.

Moisture content affects both cooking time and quality of microwaved foods. Naturally moist foods such as fresh vegetables, fish and poultry microwave more quickly and with better results than low-moisture foods such as dried beans or rice.

Size of pieces affects the cooking time. Small pieces cook faster than large ones. For even cooking, cut food into pieces of uniform size.

Shape may cause foods to cook unevenly. Chicken pieces, fish fillets and other foods which vary in thickness will take longer to cook in the thicker parts. To promote even cooking, arrange these foods with the thicker parts toward the outside of the dish where they will receive more microwave energy.

Density determines how quickly foods cook. Dense foods like roasts or whole potatoes take longer to microwave than loosely-packed foods like green beans, or porous foods like muffins.

Quantity of food in the oven directly affects microwaving time. A small amount of food cooks more quickly than a large amount, since the microwave energy is concentrated in one area.

Starting temperature of food determines how long it takes to cook or heat. Foods at room temperature cook more quickly than frozen or refrigerated foods. Hot water boils more quickly than cold, just as in conventional cooking.

Fat and bone distribution affects how evenly meats cook in the microwave oven. Well-marbled meat cooks more evenly. Large areas of fat attract energy away from the meat, and slow cooking. Boneless cuts cook more evenly, since bones conduct heat to areas near them.

MICROWAVING TECHNIQUES

Many microwave cooking techniques are similar to those used in conventional cooking. Other techniques are necessary because of the unique way microwaves cook food. In microwaving, food should be arranged and handled to allow even exposure to microwave energy. Use the techniques described here for best microwave results.

◁

Stir foods such as casseroles and vegetables at intervals during microwaving to distribute heat evenly and speed cooking. Since food at the outside of the dish absorbs more energy, stir from outside to center. Microwaved foods do not scorch or stick, so constant stirring is not necessary as in conventional cooking.

Arrange unevenly-shaped foods such as chicken pieces or salmon steaks with the thicker, meatier parts toward the outside of the dish where they will receive more microwave energy. To prevent overcooking, place delicate areas of foods such as asparagus tips toward the inside of the dish to receive less microwave energy.

Shield certain areas of food with small amounts of aluminum foil to prevent overcooking. Areas that may need shielding include quick-cooking parts of food such as the wing tips and leg ends of poultry, or areas that attract the most energy, such as the corners of square baking dishes.

Turn over foods like pork chops or baking potatoes midway during the cooking time to expose all sides to equal amounts of microwave energy. Large foods such as roasts or whole cauliflower should also be turned over to promote even cooking.

Arrange individual items such as baked potatoes or muffins in a circular pattern in the oven. This arrangement helps each item absorb an equal amount of microwave energy. Leave space between foods so that microwaves can penetrate from all sides.

Rearrange foods like meatballs or chicken pieces from the outside to the center of the dish so all pieces will receive equal exposure to microwave energy. This technique helps promote even cooking for foods which cannot be stirred. For foods like lasagna which cannot be stirred, turned over or rearranged, rotate the dish occasionally during cooking.

Let foods stand to complete cooking after they are removed from the oven. This is an important microwave technique that allows the centers of foods such as cakes, whole vegetables and roasts to complete cooking without overcooking the outer areas. Large foods build up enough internal heat to continue cooking as they stand. Length of standing time depends on the density and surface area of the food.

BROWNING

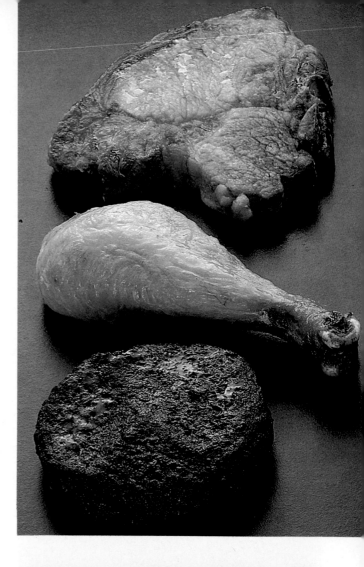

Many foods do not brown during microwaving because of the cooking speed and lack of dry heat in the microwave oven. Large cuts of meat or poultry will brown because of their fat content and longer cooking time. Bacon also browns due to its high fat content. To give microwaved foods an appearance similar to conventionally-cooked foods, use a browning agent before or during microwaving. Cakes and breads, as well as meats, can be sprinkled with toppings or crumb mixtures to add color, flavor and texture.

▷

Variations in appearance of meat are shown here, left to right: conventionally-cooked, microwaved, and microwaved with browning agent.

Browning agents can be dry or liquid, flavored or unflavored. For meats and poultry, try bouquet sauce, soy sauce, Worcestershire sauce or teriyaki sauce. Most of these should be diluted with water or butter. Dry mixtures such as soup mix or cornflake crumbs can also be used for meats. For cakes and breads, use chopped nuts, graham cracker crumbs, cinnamon-sugar or other spice mixtures.

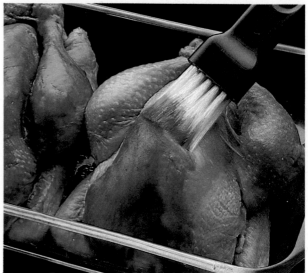

Brush or rub liquid browning agents on meats before microwaving. Dry poultry thoroughly before rubbing with diluted bouquet sauce or other browning agent. Sprinkle soup mix or other dry mixtures on meat before microwaving.

Sprinkle tops of cakes, breads or muffins with dry mixtures to add color. Cinnamon-sugar or other spice mixtures should be sprinkled on after half the cooking time. Sprinkle with chopped nuts midway or after microwaving.

Browning utensils designed especially for microwaving have a special coating on the bottom which absorbs microwaves to reach a temperature high enough to brown foods like a conventional skillet. Use these utensils for hamburgers, fried eggs, grilled sandwiches or stir-fried foods. Preheat according to manufacturer's directions.

DEFROSTING

Defrosting is one of the most helpful capabilities of your microwave oven. Microwave defrosting is much faster than refrigerator defrosting and safer than room temperature defrosting, since it does not promote the growth of harmful bacteria. POWER LEVELS **3** and **5** are generally recommended for defrosting. For best results, follow these guidelines and the directions in the charts in each section.

◁

Unwrap foods as completely as possible and place in a baking dish or on a roasting rack. Cover with wax paper to hold in warmth and help speed defrosting.

Break up or separate pieces as they defrost. Flex to break up food in pouches. Remove thawed pieces to another dish to prevent them from beginning to cook. Turn over roasts or whole poultry several times during defrosting. Shield warm areas with small pieces of foil.

Let large foods stand to complete defrosting. This allows internal heat to reach parts that are not yet defrosted. Use a wooden pick to pierce the center of meats to see if defrosting is completed. The surface should feel cool but not icy.

REHEATING

Microwave reheating makes foods taste freshly cooked—even leftovers! Reheating foods just before serving time makes meal planning and entertaining a breeze. Choose a power level appropriate to the type of food. Most kinds of food reheat best at POWER LEVEL **8**. Use the following tips to help foods reheat quickly and evenly.

▷

Arrange food on plates with thicker, denser pieces toward the outside of the plate. Spread foods like casseroles into an even layer. Test for doneness by feeling the bottom of the plate. When the plate feels warm, the food is at proper serving temperature.

Cover main dishes during reheating. If the food can be stirred, it can be reheated at HIGH. Stir occasionally during reheating to distribute heat. If the main dish cannot be stirred, reheat at a lower power level and rotate the dish during reheating.

Wrap rolls and sandwiches in paper towels before reheating to absorb moisture that may come to the surface during microwaving. Most bread products reheat in just a few seconds; to prevent toughening, do not overheat. Sugary fillings get very hot, so take care when reheating sweet rolls.

CONVERTING CONVENTIONAL RECIPES

Many of your favorite conventional recipes can be converted for the microwave oven by just shortening the cooking time. Other recipes may require changing the amount of seasoning, liquid or fat. Check a microwave recipe similar to the one you are converting and compare ingredients. Study the following techniques to help you convert recipes successfully.

Select recipes for foods which microwave well. Casseroles and other main dishes that are cooked in a sauce adapt particularly well. Look for conventional techniques such as covering, steaming or braising. Recipes with these techniques can usually be converted with good results.

Use slightly less seasoning, especially salt and highly-flavored seasonings such as garlic, curry powder and cayenne. Correct the seasoning to taste after microwaving. Small amounts of mild seasonings do not need to be adjusted.

Reduce liquid to about three-fourths of the amount the conventional recipe calls for when simmering or baking. Little evaporation occurs during microwaving, so less liquid is needed. If necessary, add more liquid as you cook.

Do not convert recipes for deep-fried foods or those which require a dry, crusty surface. These include French fries, popovers, pancakes, pizza and two-crust pies. Yeast breads can be baked in the microwave, but they must be made from a recipe specially developed for microwaving.

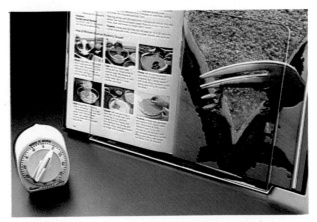

Estimate microwave time by using a microwave recipe as a guide, or by reducing conventional cooking time by one-fourth to one-third. Check for doneness after the minimum time and add more time in small amounts. Quantity affects time, so increase time when doubling a recipe.

Omit fat needed to brown foods or prevent sticking. Small amounts of butter or oil can be used for flavoring, but are otherwise not necessary—a plus for the calorie-conscious or those who need to watch cholesterol intake.

Moist foods such as chicken, seafood, and vegetables adapt well to microwaving. These foods cook successfully without the dry heat of conventional cooking. Most require less added moisture than the conventional recipe calls for.

TIPS & IDEAS

Melt butter for recipes or popcorn in a glass measure or small bowl at HIGH. No need to dirty a pan.

Soften cream cheese at POWER LEVEL **5** for dips, spreads and other recipes. No need to wait for it to soften at room temperature.

Melt chocolate in a custard cup or glass measure at POWER LEVEL **5**. Clean-up is easy and there's less chance of scorching.

Soften brown sugar by placing an apple slice in the bag or box and microwaving at HIGH for a few seconds to soften lumps.

Plump raisins by sprinkling with 1 or 2 teaspoons water. Cover and microwave at HIGH for 30 to 60 seconds.

Get more juice from citrus fruits by microwaving whole at HIGH for a few seconds before cutting and squeezing.

TIPS & IDEAS

Start ribs or chicken in the microwave and finish them on the charcoal grill for barbecued flavor without the wait.

Grill extra hamburgers, undercooking slightly. Freeze them, then reheat in the microwave for grilled flavor another time.

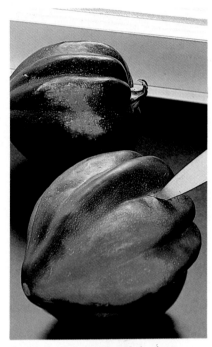

Soften acorn squash before cutting to make the task easier. Pierce with a knife, microwave at HIGH until just warm to the touch, then cut.

Remove nuts from shells which are difficult to remove whole, like Brazil nuts and filberts. Microwave 8 oz. nuts in 1 cup water at HIGH for 4 to 5 minutes, then remove shells.

Warm towels for an Oriental touch at dinner. Place dampened washcloths in a dish or basket, and microwave at HIGH until just warm.

Refresh the oven by placing ½ cup water in a 4-cup measure. Add 2 slices lemon. Microwave at HIGH until water boils, then 1 minute longer.

APPETIZERS

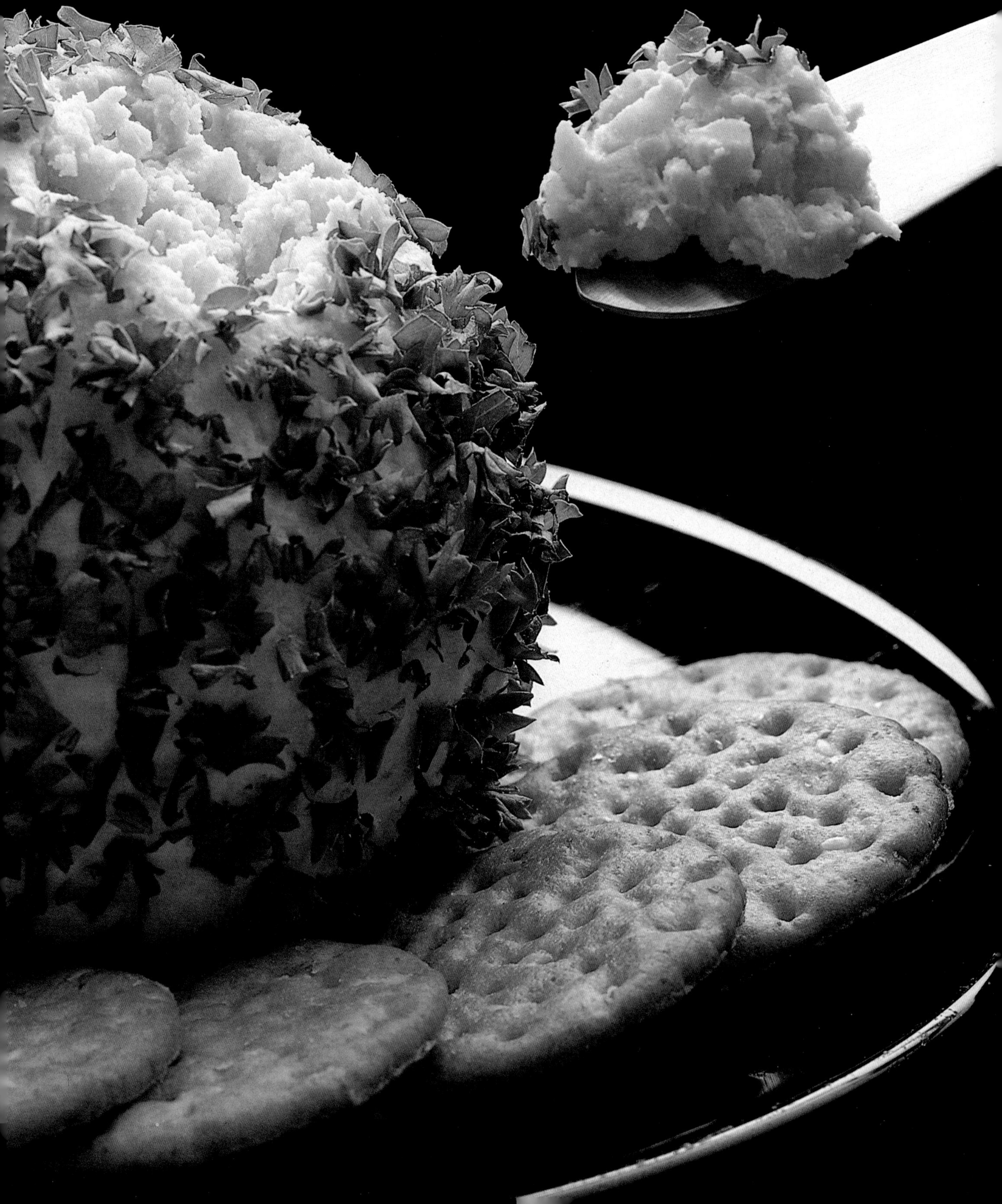

APPETIZER PÂTÉ △

Power Levels / HIGH, **7**
Approx. Cooking Time / 7 minutes
Yield / About 1½ cups

¼ cup butter or margarine
1 lb. chicken livers, drained
½ cup chicken broth
⅓ cup chopped onion
¼ teaspoon dried thyme leaves
4 slices bacon, cooked and crumbled, page 63
1 tablespoon sherry (optional)
½ teaspoon garlic salt
   Dash pepper
½ to 1 teaspoon dried parsley flakes
   Assorted crackers

1 Place butter in small bowl. Microwave at
   HIGH for 10 to 20 seconds, or until butter
   softens. Set aside.

2 In 1-quart casserole, combine livers, broth,
   onion and thyme. Cover. Microwave at HIGH
   for 3 minutes.

3 Reduce to POWER LEVEL **7**. Microwave for
   3 to 4 minutes longer, or until livers are no
   longer pink. Drain, reserving ¼ cup liquid.

4 In food processor or blender pitcher, combine
   liver mixture, reserved liquid, bacon, sherry,
   garlic salt, pepper and softened butter. Blend
   until smooth.

5 Transfer mixture to small bowl. Sprinkle with
   parsley flakes. Cover and refrigerate for at least
   8 hours. Serve with crackers.

STUFFED MUSHROOMS

Power Level / HIGH
Approx. Cooking Time / 14 minutes
Yield / 6 to 8 servings

2 slices bacon
8 oz. fresh medium mushrooms
¼ cup chopped onion
3 tablespoons seasoned dry bread crumbs
1 tablespoon grated Parmesan cheese
⅛ teaspoon salt
   Dash pepper

1 Place bacon in small mixing bowl. Microwave
   at HIGH for 2 to 3 minutes, or until crisp.
   Remove bacon, reserving drippings. Drain
   bacon on paper towels; set aside.

2 Remove caps from mushrooms; set aside.
   Chop stems. Add chopped stems and onion
   to reserved bacon drippings. Microwave at
   HIGH for 2½ to 3½ minutes, or until onion
   is tender.

3 Crumble bacon into mushroom mixture. Stir
   in bread crumbs, Parmesan cheese, salt and
   pepper. Stuff small amount of mixture into
   each mushroom cap.

4 Place stuffed mushroom caps on paper towel-
   lined plate or paper plate. Microwave at
   HIGH for 6 to 8 minutes, or until hot, rotating
   plate once.

COCKTAIL REUBENS ▽

Power Level / **7**
Approx. Cooking Time / 8 minutes
Yield / 36 appetizers

36 slices cocktail rye bread, toasted
½ cup Thousand Island dressing
1 can (8 oz.) sauerkraut, rinsed and drained
¼ lb. thinly-sliced corned beef
1 pkg. (6 oz.) Swiss cheese slices, each cut into
**   4 squares**

1 Arrange 9 slices bread on paper towel-lined plate or paper plate. Spread each slice with about ¾ teaspoon Thousand Island dressing. Add small amount of sauerkraut and corned beef to each slice. Top each with 1 square Swiss cheese.

2 Microwave at POWER LEVEL **7** for 1½ to 2 minutes, or until cheese melts, rotating plate 1 or 2 times. Repeat with remaining ingredients.

CHEESE BALL

Power Levels / HIGH, **5**, **1**
Approx. Cooking Time / 6 minutes
Yield / One 4-inch cheese ball

¼ cup butter or margarine
1 pkg. (3 oz.) cream cheese
1 teaspoon Worcestershire sauce
½ teaspoon onion powder
⅛ teaspoon garlic powder
3 cups shredded Cheddar cheese (about 12 oz.)
½ cup finely-chopped walnuts or snipped
      fresh parsley
   Assorted crackers

1 Place butter in small bowl. Microwave at
   HIGH for 10 to 20 seconds, or until
   butter softens.

2 Place cream cheese in medium mixing bowl.
   Microwave at POWER LEVEL **5** for 30 to 60
   seconds, or until cream cheese softens.

3 Blend in softened butter, Worcestershire sauce,
   onion powder and garlic powder. Stir in
   Cheddar cheese. Microwave at POWER
   LEVEL **1** for 5 minutes.

4 Beat at medium speed of electric mixer until
   smooth. Shape into ball. Roll in nuts to coat.
   Wrap in plastic wrap. Refrigerate for at least
   3 hours. Serve with crackers.

CURRIED ALMONDS

Power Level / HIGH
Approx. Cooking Time / 6 minutes
Yield / 2 cups

2 tablespoons butter or margarine
1 to 2 tablespoons curry powder
1 tablespoon Worcestershire sauce
1 cup blanched whole almonds (about 4 oz.)
1 cup unblanched whole almonds (about 4 oz.)

1 Place butter in 9-inch round baking dish.
   Microwave at HIGH for 45 to 60 seconds, or
   until butter melts.

2 Stir in curry powder and Worcestershire
   sauce. Add blanched and unblanched
   almonds. Stir to coat. Microwave at HIGH for
   4 to 5 minutes, or until blanched almonds are
   golden brown, stirring once.

GARLIC SHRIMP ▷

Power Levels / HIGH, **7**
Approx. Cooking Time / 3 minutes
Yield / 2 to 4 servings

2 tablespoons butter or margarine
2 cloves garlic, minced
¼ lb. fresh medium shrimp, peeled and
      deveined, opposite
1½ teaspoons snipped fresh parsley
1½ teaspoons grated Parmesan cheese

1 In 1-quart casserole, combine butter and
   garlic. Microwave at HIGH for 1 to 1½
   minutes, or until garlic lightly browns.

2 Stir in shrimp and parsley. Microwave at
   POWER LEVEL **7** for 1 to 1½ minutes, or until
   shrimp are firm and opaque, stirring once.

3 Stir in Parmesan cheese. Use wooden picks or
   cocktail forks for easy serving.

TANGY SHRIMP

Power Levels / HIGH, **7**
Approx. Cooking Time / 18 minutes
Yield / 4 to 6 servings

½ cup chili sauce
½ cup sweet pickle relish
½ cup beer
½ lb. fresh medium shrimp, peeled and
      deveined, opposite

1 In 1½-quart casserole, mix chili sauce, pickle
   relish and beer. Microwave at HIGH for 3 to 4
   minutes, or until hot and bubbly, stirring once.

2 Reduce to POWER LEVEL **7**. Microwave for
   10 minutes longer, or until mixture thickens,
   stirring 2 or 3 times.

3 Stir in shrimp. Microwave at POWER LEVEL
   7 for 3 to 4 minutes, or until shrimp are firm
   and opaque, stirring once. Cover. Let stand for
   2 minutes. Use wooden picks or cocktail forks
   for easy serving.

HOW TO PEEL AND DEVEIN SHRIMP

LOOSEN shell on the underside of shrimp. Remove shell, leaving tail intact if desired.

CUT down middle of back from tail to thick end. With point of a knife, loosen and remove vein.

ITALIAN VEGETABLES △

Power Level / HIGH
Approx. Cooking Time / 7 minutes
Yield / About 4 cups

1 cup green pepper pieces, 1-inch pieces
1 cup sliced carrot, ¼-inch slices
1 cup fresh cauliflowerets
1 cup fresh broccoli flowerets
½ cup Italian dressing

1 In medium mixing bowl, combine green
  pepper, carrot, cauliflower and broccoli. Add
  dressing. Toss to coat vegetables. Cover bowl
  with plastic wrap.

2 Microwave at HIGH for 6 to 7 minutes, or until
  vegetables are tender-crisp, stirring once.
  Refrigerate for at least 3 hours before serving.

CHEESE 'N BACON STICKS △

Power Level / HIGH
Approx. Cooking Time / 5 minutes
Yield / 8 appetizers

4 slices bacon
8 cheese-flavored bread sticks

1 Assemble appetizers according to photo
  directions below.

2 Microwave at HIGH for 4 to 5 minutes, or until
  bacon is crisp, rotating rack once. Let stand for
  1 to 2 minutes.

HOW TO ASSEMBLE CHEESE 'N BACON STICKS

CUT each bacon slice in half lengthwise. Wrap 1
bacon strip around each bread stick to form a
spiral pattern.

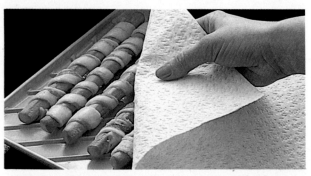

ARRANGE appetizers on roasting rack. Cover
with paper towel. Microwave as directed in step
2 above.

CRAB MEAT SUPREME

Power Levels / 5, 7
Approx. Cooking Time / 5 minutes
Yield / 32 appetizers

1 pkg. (3 oz.) cream cheese
1 can (6 oz.) crab meat, rinsed, cleaned and flaked
¼ cup finely-chopped celery
1 tablespoon finely-chopped green onion
2 teaspoons prepared mustard
Dash cayenne
32 melba cracker rounds

1 Place cream cheese in medium mixing bowl.
Microwave at POWER LEVEL 5 for 30 to 60
seconds, or until cream cheese softens.
Add remaining ingredients except crackers.
Mix well.

2 Spread about 1 tablespoon crab meat mixture
on each cracker. Arrange 8 crackers on paper
towel-lined plate or paper plate. Microwave at
POWER LEVEL 7 for 45 to 60 seconds, or
until hot, rotating plate once. Repeat with
remaining crackers.

MEXICALI PARTY DIP

Power Level / 5
Approx. Cooking Time / 7 minutes
Yield / About 3 cups

1 can (16 oz.) whole tomatoes, drained and
chopped
1 can (4 oz.) chopped green chilies
1 lb. process cheese spread, shredded
Dash hot pepper sauce
Taco or tortilla chips

1 In 2-quart casserole, combine tomatoes,
chilies, cheese and hot pepper sauce.

2 Microwave at POWER LEVEL 5 for 7
minutes, or until cheese melts, stirring every
2 minutes. Serve with chips.

HOT MEXICALI PARTY DIP

Follow recipe above, substituting 1 can (4 oz.)
chopped jalapeño peppers, drained, for
green chilies.

HAM ROLL-UPS

Power Level / 7
Approx. Cooking Time / 5 minutes
Yield / 24 appetizers

6 thin slices ham (about 1 oz. each)
1 tablespoon prepared brown mustard
6 slices process American cheese food
(about 1 oz. each)

1 Spread each slice of ham with small amount of
mustard. Top each with 1 cheese slice. Roll up
jelly roll-style, starting at shorter end. Cut
each roll into quarters. Secure each roll-up
with wooden pick.

2 Arrange 12 roll-ups on plate. Microwave at
POWER LEVEL 7 for 2 to 2½ minutes, or
until cheese melts, rotating plate once.
Repeat with remaining roll-ups.

TEXAS-STYLE NACHOS

Power Level / 7
Approx. Cooking Time / 5 minutes
Yield / 20 appetizers

20 taco or tortilla chips
½ cup bean dip
½ cup guacamole dip
20 thin slices canned jalapeño pepper
1½ cups shredded Monterey Jack cheese
(about 6 oz.)

1 Arrange 10 chips on paper towel-lined plate or
paper plate. Spread each chip with about
1 teaspoon bean dip. Top each with about
1 teaspoon guacamole dip and 1 jalapeño
pepper slice. Sprinkle chips with half the
Monterey Jack cheese.

2 Microwave at POWER LEVEL 7 for 2 to 2½
minutes, or until cheese melts, rotating plate
1 or 2 times. Repeat with remaining chips.

SOUPS,
SANDWICHES
& BEVERAGES

CREAM OF SPINACH SOUP

Power Levels / HIGH, **7**
Approx. Cooking Time / 21 minutes
Yield / 4 to 6 servings

1 pkg. (10 oz.) frozen chopped spinach
6 tablespoons butter or margarine
1 tablespoon finely-chopped onion
5 tablespoons all-purpose flour
¾ teaspoon salt
  Dash pepper
  Dash ground nutmeg (optional)
2 cups milk
1 cup chicken broth

1 Remove spinach from packaging and place on plate. Microwave at HIGH for 4 to 5 minutes. Let stand for 5 to 10 minutes. Press to remove excess moisture.

2 In 2-quart casserole, combine butter and onion. Microwave at HIGH for 1½ to 2 minutes, or until onion is tender-crisp.

3 Stir in flour, salt, pepper and nutmeg. Blend in milk and broth. Microwave at POWER LEVEL **7** for 8 to 10 minutes, or until mixture thickens, stirring occasionally.

4 Stir in spinach. Microwave at POWER LEVEL **7** for 3 to 4 minutes, or until heated through, stirring once.

CREAM OF BROCCOLI SOUP ▽

Follow recipe above, substituting 1 pkg. (10 oz.) frozen chopped broccoli for spinach.

NEW ENGLAND CLAM CHOWDER △

Power Level / HIGH
Approx. Cooking Time / 22 minutes
Yield / 4 servings

4 slices bacon
2 medium white potatoes, peeled and diced
¼ cup finely-chopped onion
3 tablespoons all-purpose flour
1 teaspoon salt
¼ teaspoon dried thyme leaves
⅛ teaspoon pepper
1 can (6½ oz.) minced clams
2 cups milk

1 Place bacon in 2-quart casserole. Microwave at HIGH for 3 to 4 minutes, or until crisp. Remove bacon, reserving drippings. Drain bacon on paper towels; set aside.

2 Stir potatoes and onion into bacon drippings. Cover. Microwave at HIGH for 7 to 10 minutes, or until potatoes are tender, stirring every 3 minutes.

3 Stir in flour, salt, thyme and pepper. Drain clams, reserving juice. Blend clam juice and milk into potato mixture. Microwave at HIGH for 7 to 8 minutes, or until mixture thickens, stirring every 2 minutes. Crumble bacon into mixture. Stir in clams.

RUSSIAN BORSCHT △

Power Level / HIGH
Approx. Cooking Time / 11 minutes
Yield / 4 or 5 servings

½ **cup finely-chopped onion**
2 **tablespoons butter or margarine**
1 **can (16 oz.) diced beets, drained**
1 **cup hot water**
1 **tablespoon instant beef bouillon granules**
1 **cup hot water**
  Dash hot pepper sauce
  Dairy sour cream

1 In 2-quart casserole, combine onion and
   butter. Microwave at HIGH for 3 to 5 minutes,
   or until onion is tender, stirring once.

2 Transfer onion and butter to blender pitcher.
   Add beets, 1 cup hot water and the bouillon
   granules. Blend until smooth. Transfer back to
   2-quart casserole.

3 Stir in 1 cup hot water and the hot pepper
   sauce. Microwave at HIGH for 5 to 6 minutes,
   or until hot. Serve with sour cream.

VEGETABLE BEEF SOUP △

Power Level / HIGH
Approx. Cooking Time / 18 minutes
Yield / 4 or 5 servings

½ **lb. ground beef**
¾ **cup thinly-sliced celery**
¼ **cup finely-chopped onion**
1 **medium carrot, shredded**
1 **can (16 oz.) whole tomatoes, undrained, cut up**
1 **can (14½ oz.) beef broth**
¾ **teaspoon salt**
1 **bay leaf**
¼ **teaspoon dried marjoram leaves**
⅛ **teaspoon pepper**
⅛ **teaspoon dried thyme leaves**

1 Place ground beef in 2-quart casserole.
   Microwave at HIGH for 2 to 2½ minutes, or
   until beef is no longer pink, stirring
   once. Drain.

2 Add celery, onion and carrot. Cover.
   Microwave at HIGH for 3 to 4 minutes, or until
   vegetables are tender, stirring once.

3 Stir in remaining ingredients. Re-cover.
   Microwave at HIGH for 10 to 12 minutes, or
   until hot. Remove and discard bay leaf.

HAM AND VEGETABLE CHOWDER △

Power Levels / HIGH, **7**
Approx. Cooking Time / 20 minutes
Yield / 6 to 8 servings

½ **cup thinly-sliced celery**
3 **tablespoons butter or margarine**
1 **can (10¾ oz.) condensed cream of celery soup**
1 **can (10¾ oz.) condensed cream of onion soup**
2½ **cups milk**
1 **pkg. (10 oz.) frozen mixed vegetables**
1 **cup cubed fully-cooked ham, ½-inch cubes**

1 In 2-quart casserole, combine celery and butter. Microwave at HIGH for 3 to 4 minutes, or until celery is tender.

2 Blend in celery soup, onion soup and milk. Add vegetables and ham. Cover. Microwave at POWER LEVEL **7** for 11 to 16 minutes, or until hot, stirring 1 or 2 times.

SPLIT PEA SOUP △

Power Levels / HIGH, **5**
Approx. Cooking Time / 1 hour 15 minutes
Yield / 8 to 10 servings

6 **cups hot water**
1 **pkg. (16 oz.) dried split peas, sorted**
½ **lb. bacon, chopped**
1 **cup chopped celery**
½ **cup chopped onion**
½ **cup thinly-sliced carrots**
1 **teaspoon salt**
⅛ **teaspoon dried thyme leaves**
⅛ **teaspoon pepper**

1 In 5-quart casserole, mix all ingredients. Cover. Microwave at HIGH for 10 minutes.

2 Reduce to POWER LEVEL **5**. Microwave for 55 to 65 minutes longer, or until peas are tender, stirring occasionally.

3 Remove 2 cups soup. Mash with fork. Add back to soup. Add additional hot water for thinner soup, if desired.

HAM AND SPLIT PEA SOUP

Follow recipe above, substituting 1 ham bone for bacon. Before mashing 2 cups soup, remove bone. Cut meat from bone and stir into soup. Discard bone and fat. Continue as directed.

◁

CHICKEN GUMBO

Power Level / HIGH
Approx. Cooking Time / 36 minutes
Yield / 6 to 8 servings

2½ to 3-lb. broiler-fryer chicken, cut up
  1 medium onion, sliced
  1 tablespoon all-purpose flour
  1 can (16 oz.) stewed tomatoes
  1 pkg. (10 oz.) frozen sliced okra
  1 can (8 oz.) whole kernel corn, drained
1½ teaspoons instant chicken bouillon granules
  ½ teaspoon salt
  ⅛ teaspoon garlic powder
  ⅛ teaspoon pepper
  5 or 6 drops hot pepper sauce

1 Place chicken in 3-quart casserole. Cover.
Microwave at HIGH for 10 to 12 minutes, or
until meat near bone is no longer pink and
juices run clear, turning over and rearranging
after half the time. Remove chicken from
cooking liquid and set aside.

2 Skim and discard fat from cooking liquid.
Pour liquid into 2-cup measure. Add enough
water to make 2 cups. Set aside. Remove
chicken meat from skin and bones. Discard
skin and bones. Cut meat into bite-size pieces.

3 Place onion in 3-quart casserole. Cover.
Microwave at HIGH for 4 to 5 minutes, or until
tender, stirring once.

4 Blend in flour. Stir in reserved 2 cups liquid,
the chicken and remaining ingredients. Cover.
Microwave at HIGH for 3 to 4 minutes, or until
okra slices can be stirred apart. Microwave
for 10 to 15 minutes longer, or until hot,
stirring once.

CHEESE 'N BACON HOT DOGS ▽

Power Level / HIGH
Approx. Cooking Time / 5 minutes
Yield / 4 sandwiches

4 wieners
1 slice process American cheese food (about ¾ oz.),
    cut into 8 strips
4 slices bacon
4 hot dog buns

1 Make lengthwise slit almost all the way
through each wiener, cutting to within ½ inch
of each end. Place 2 strips cheese in each slit.

2 Arrange bacon on 3 layers of paper towels.
Cover with another paper towel. Microwave at
HIGH for 3 minutes.

3 Quickly wrap 1 bacon slice around each
wiener. Secure with wooden picks. Arrange
wieners on plate. Microwave at HIGH for
1½ to 2 minutes, or until cheese begins to
melt. Serve in buns.

TUNA MELTS

Power Level / ⑦
Approx. Cooking Time / 4 minutes
Yield / 4 sandwiches

1 can (6½ oz.) tuna, drained and flaked
⅓ cup mayonnaise or salad dressing
¼ teaspoon onion powder
⅛ teaspoon celery seed
⅛ teaspoon pepper
⅛ teaspoon salt
4 slices whole wheat or white bread, toasted
4 thin slices tomato
4 slices process American cheese food
    (about ¾ oz. each)

1 In small mixing bowl, combine tuna,
mayonnaise, onion powder, celery seed,
pepper and salt. Mix well. Divide and
spread mixture evenly on bread slices. Top
each sandwich with 1 tomato slice and 1
cheese slice.

2 Place sandwiches on paper towel-lined plate
or paper plate. Microwave at POWER LEVEL
⑦ for 3½ to 4 minutes, or until cheese melts,
rotating plate 2 times.

REUBEN DELI MELTS △

Power Levels / **9**, **7**
Approx. Cooking Time / 3 minutes
Yield / 4 sandwiches

½ lb. thinly-sliced corned beef
8 slices rye or pumpernickel bread, toasted*
4 tablespoons Thousand Island dressing
1 can (8 oz.) sauerkraut, rinsed and drained
4 slices (7 x 4 inches) natural Swiss cheese (1 to 1½
   oz. each), cut in half

1 Divide corned beef evenly among 4 bread
   slices. Spread corned beef with dressing.
   Top sandwiches with sauerkraut.

2 Arrange sandwiches on paper towel-lined
   plate or paper plate. Microwave at POWER
   LEVEL **9** for 1½ minutes, or until corned beef
   is warm.

3 Top each sandwich with 2 halves Swiss
   cheese. Microwave at POWER LEVEL **7** for
   1½ to 2 minutes, or until cheese melts, rotating
   plate once. Top with remaining bread slices or
   serve open-face.

*For open-face sandwiches, use 4 slices bread.

HAM, CHEESE AND APPLE SANDWICHES △

Power Levels / **9**, **7**
Approx. Cooking Time / 3 minutes
Yield / 4 sandwiches

8 slices raisin bread, toasted*
2 to 3 teaspoons prepared mustard
½ lb. thinly-sliced fully-cooked ham
½ medium apple, thinly sliced
4 slices process American cheese food
   (about ¾ oz. each)

1 Spread 4 bread slices with small amount of
   mustard. Arrange on paper towel-lined plate
   or paper plate. Divide half of ham evenly
   among bread. Add a few apple slices to each
   sandwich. Top with remaining half of ham.
   Microwave at POWER LEVEL **9** for 2
   minutes, or until heated through.

2 Add 1 cheese slice to each sandwich.
   Microwave at POWER LEVEL **7** for 1 to 1½
   minutes, or until cheese melts. Top with
   remaining bread slices or serve open-face.

*For open-face sandwiches, use 4 slices bread.

PIZZA SUBS ▷

Power Levels / HIGH, **7**
Approx. Cooking Time / 9 minutes
Yield / 8 sandwiches

½ lb. ground beef
¼ cup finely-chopped onion
½ cup pizza sauce
¼ teaspoon salt
¼ teaspoon dried oregano leaves
4 Italian or French rolls (about 6 inches long), split
    in half lengthwise and toasted
1 can (4 oz.) sliced mushrooms, drained
    Sliced pepperoni (optional)
    Green pepper slices (optional)
1½ cups shredded mozzarella cheese (about 6 oz.)

1 In 1-quart casserole, combine ground beef
  and onion. Microwave at HIGH for 2½ to 3½
  minutes, or until beef is no longer pink,
  stirring once. Drain.

2 Stir in pizza sauce, salt and oregano.
  Microwave at HIGH for 2 minutes, or until
  flavors are blended, stirring once.

3 Arrange rolls, cut-side up, on paper towel-
  lined plate or paper plate. Divide and spread
  beef mixture evenly on rolls. Top with
  mushrooms, pepperoni and green pepper.
  Sprinkle with mozzarella cheese.

4 Microwave at POWER LEVEL **7** for 3 to 4
  minutes, or until cheese melts, rotating
  plate once.

<u>TIP</u> ▪ Top Pizza Subs with your own combination
of ingredients. Try cooked Italian sausage or
Canadian bacon. Add chopped black or pimiento-
stuffed olives, tomato slices, anchovies or onions to
add flavor and variety.

SLOPPY JOES △

Power Levels / HIGH, **7**
Approx. Cooking Time / 10 minutes
Yield / 4 sandwiches

 1 lb. ground beef
⅓ cup finely-chopped onion
¼ cup finely-chopped celery
½ cup ketchup
 1 tablespoon prepared mustard
 1 tablespoon water
 2 teaspoons packed brown sugar
½ teaspoon salt
½ teaspoon chili powder
⅛ to ¼ teaspoon cayenne
 4 hamburger buns

1 In 1-quart casserole, combine ground beef,
   onion and celery. Microwave at HIGH for 4 to
   5 minutes, or until beef is no longer pink,
   stirring once. Drain.

2 Stir in remaining ingredients except buns.
   Cover. Microwave at POWER LEVEL **7** for 5
   minutes, or until mixture is hot and flavors are
   blended. Divide evenly among buns.

CREAMY COCOA △

Power Level / **7**
Approx. Cooking Time / 12 minutes
Yield / 6 servings

½ cup packed brown sugar
⅓ cup cocoa
 1 teaspoon vanilla
½ teaspoon salt
 5 cups milk
   Whipped cream (optional)

1 In 2-quart measure or medium mixing bowl,
   combine brown sugar, cocoa, vanilla and salt.
   Gradually blend in milk, stirring until sugar is
   dissolved. Microwave at POWER LEVEL **7** for
   10 to 12 minutes, or until temperature reaches
   150°F,* stirring 2 times.

2 Pour into serving cups. Top with dollop
   whipped cream.

MOCHA COCOA

Follow recipe above, adding 1 tablespoon instant
coffee crystals to dry ingredients.

*Use temperature probe, if desired.

BEVERAGE MICROWAVING GUIDE

ITEM	TOTAL COOKING TIME	FINAL TEMPERATURE*	POWER LEVEL
Water (for instant coffee or tea)			
One 6-oz. cup	1½ to 2½ min.	190°F	HIGH
Two 6-oz. cups	2½ to 3½ min.	190°F	
Milk (for hot cocoa)			
One 6-oz. cup	1½ to 2½ min.	150°F	**7**
Two 6-oz. cups	2½ to 3½ min.	150°F	

*Use temperature probe, if desired.

CRANBERRY WARMER

Power Level / HIGH
Approx. Cooking Time / 4 minutes
Yield / 4 servings

3 cups cranberry or cranberry-apple juice cocktail
2 tablespoons honey
4 sticks cinnamon
8 whole allspice
8 whole cloves

1 In 4-cup measure or medium mixing bowl, combine all ingredients. Microwave at HIGH for 3½ to 4½ minutes, or until temperature reaches 150°F,* stirring once.

2 Strain and pour into serving cups.

*Use temperature probe, if desired.

MULLED CIDER

Power Level / HIGH
Approx. Cooking Time / 4 minutes
Yield / 4 or 5 servings

4 cups apple juice
2 sticks cinnamon
4 whole cloves
⅛ teaspoon ground nutmeg

1 In 2-quart measure or medium mixing bowl, combine all ingredients. Microwave at HIGH for 3½ to 4½ minutes, or until temperature reaches 150°F.*

2 Strain and pour into serving cups.

*Use temperature probe, if desired.

TIPS FOR MICROWAVING BEVERAGES

PREPARE beverages in a bowl with a pouring spout so drinks can be easily served without spilling. A 4-cup or 2-quart glass measure is ideal. Use a long-handled ladle to serve beverages if you don't have a bowl with a spout.

SIMPLIFY cleanup by mixing and heating beverages right in the serving container. Mugs, pitchers and small punch bowls can be used if they are microwave-safe. Be sure there are no metallic handles or trim.

HOT BUTTERED RUM △

Power Level / HIGH
Approx. Cooking Time / 4 minutes
Yield / 4 servings

2⅔ cups apple cider
  4 tablespoons packed brown sugar
  4 sticks cinnamon
  ¾ cup rum
  4 teaspoons butter or margarine
    Ground nutmeg

1 Pour ⅔ cup cider into each of 4 serving cups.
   Stir 1 tablespoon brown sugar into each cup.
   Add 1 cinnamon stick to each. Microwave
   at HIGH for 3½ to 4½ minutes, or until
   temperature reaches 150°F.*

2 Stir 3 tablespoons rum, 1 teaspoon butter and
   a dash nutmeg into each cup.

*Use temperature probe, if desired.

HOT BUTTERSCOTCH △

Power Level / **7**
Approx. Cooking Time / 12 minutes
Yield / 4 to 6 servings

¼ cup milk
½ cup butterscotch chips
3¾ cups milk
¼ teaspoon ground cinnamon
    Miniature marshmallows

1 In 2-quart measure or medium mixing bowl,
   combine ¼ cup milk and the butterscotch
   chips. Microwave at POWER LEVEL **7** for
   2½ to 3½ minutes, or until chips melt,
   stirring once.

2 Blend in 3¾ cups milk and the cinnamon.
   Microwave at POWER LEVEL **7** for 7 to 9
   minutes, or until temperature reaches 150°F,*
   stirring once. Pour into serving cups. Top with
   marshmallows.

*Use temperature probe, if desired.

ORANGE WARM-UP △

Power Level / HIGH
Approx. Cooking Time / 5 minutes
Yield / 4 or 5 servings

3 cups apricot nectar
1 cup orange juice
2 sticks cinnamon
1 teaspoon whole cloves
4 thin slices orange (optional)

1 In 2-quart measure or medium mixing bowl, combine all ingredients except orange slices. Microwave at HIGH for 4½ to 5½ minutes, or until temperature reaches 150°F.*

2 Strain and pour into serving cups. Garnish with orange slices.

*Use temperature probe, if desired.

APRICOT TEA △

Power Levels / HIGH, **7**
Approx. Cooking Time / 8 minutes
Yield / 4 servings

3 cups water
4 tea bags
4 tablespoons apricot preserves
4 tablespoons apricot brandy (optional)
Whipped cream (optional)
Ground nutmeg (optional)

1 Pour ¾ cup water into each of 4 serving cups. Microwave at HIGH for about 3 minutes, or until water is hot.

2 Place 1 tea bag in each cup. Microwave at POWER LEVEL **7** for 3 to 5 minutes, or until tea is desired strength. Remove and discard tea bags.

3 Stir 1 tablespoon preserves and 1 tablespoon brandy into each cup. Top with dollop whipped cream and dash nutmeg.

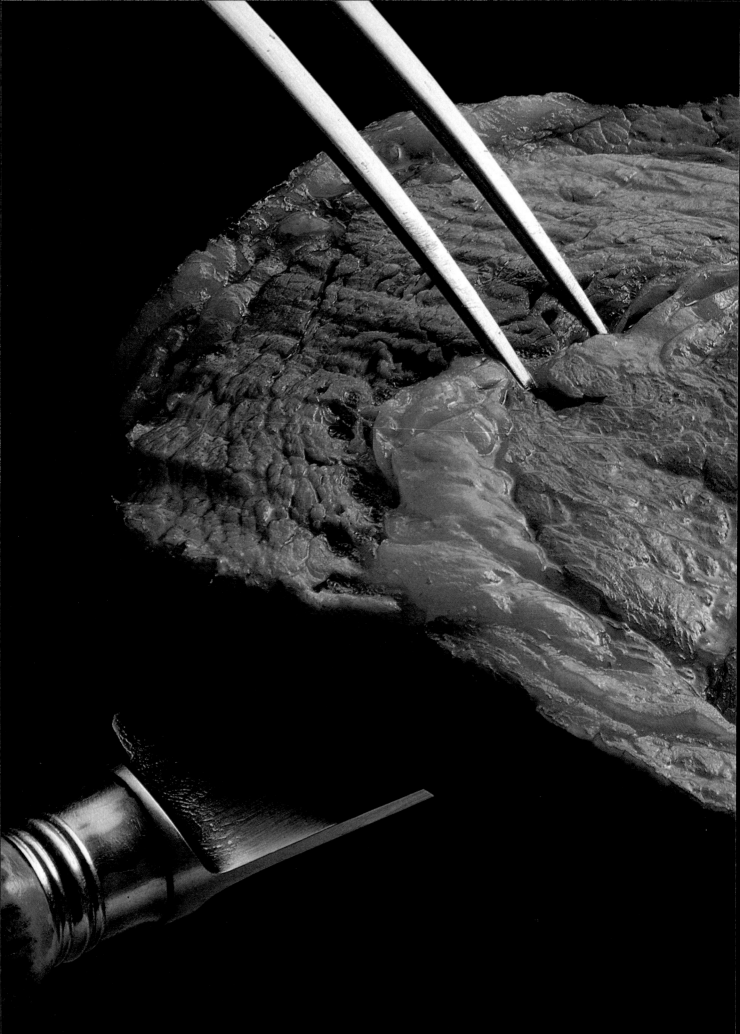

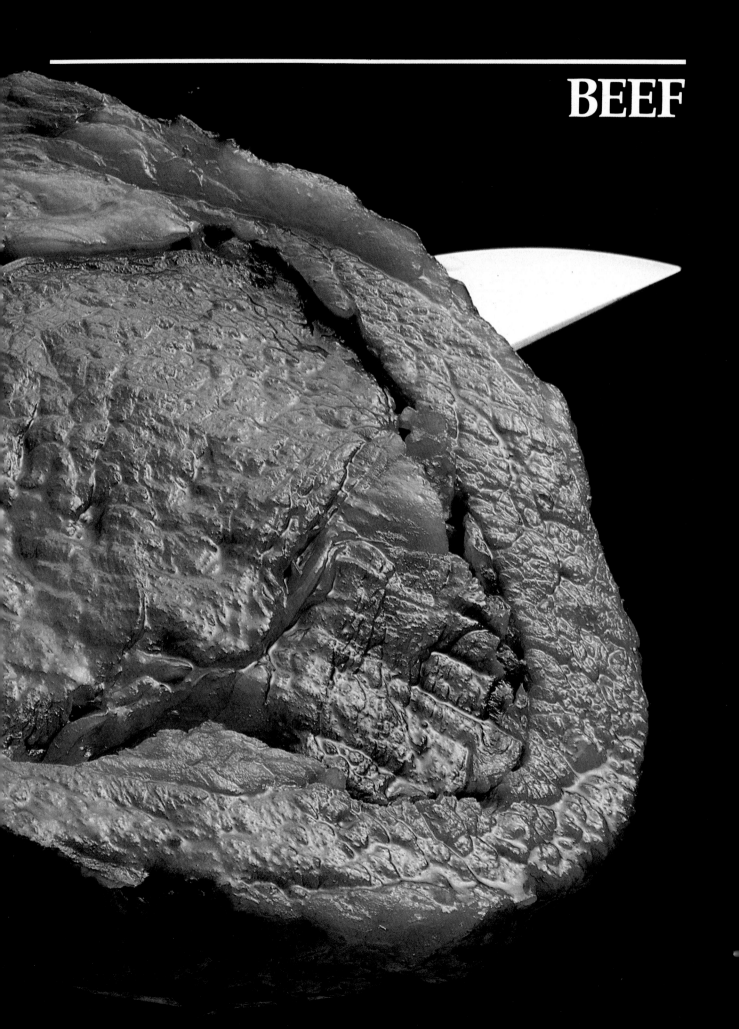

BEEF

BEEF DEFROSTING GUIDE

ITEM	TOTAL DEFROSTING TIME	POWER LEVEL	METHOD
Roast boneless	9 to 11 min./lb.	**3**	Remove packaging. Place roast on roasting rack. Microwave until wooden pick can be easily inserted in center, turning over after half the time.* Let stand for 10 to 15 min.
bone-in	9 to 11 min./lb.	**3**	Same as above.
Chuck Roast	9 to 11 min./lb.	**3**	Remove packaging. Place roast on roasting rack. Microwave until wooden pick can be easily inserted in center, turning over after half the time.* Let stand for 10 to 15 min.
Steaks	4 to 7 min./lb.	**5**	Remove packaging. Place steaks on roasting rack. Microwave until pliable, breaking apart and rearranging as soon as possible.* Let stand for 10 to 15 min.
Short Ribs	5 to 8 min./lb.	**5**	Remove packaging. Place ribs on roasting rack. Microwave until pliable, breaking apart and rearranging as soon as possible.* Let stand for 10 to 15 min.
Liver, sliced	9 to 11 min./lb.	**3**	Remove packaging. Place liver on roasting rack. Microwave until pliable, breaking apart and rearranging as soon as possible.* Let stand for 10 to 15 min.
Stew Meat	5 to 7 min./lb.	**5**	Remove packaging. Place beef on plate. Microwave until wooden pick can be easily inserted in each piece, breaking apart and rearranging as soon as possible. Let stand for 5 to 10 min.
Hamburger Patties, ¼ lb. each, ½ inch thick 2 patties 4 patties	1½ to 2½ min. 4 to 5 min.	**5**	Remove packaging. Break patties apart, if possible. Arrange on plate. Microwave until wooden pick can be easily inserted in each patty, turning over after half the time. Let stand for 5 to 10 min.
Ground Beef	4 to 6 min./lb.	**5**	Remove packaging. Place beef on plate. Microwave breaking apart and removing defrosted portions as soon as possible. Let stand for 5 to 10 min.

*Shield warm areas as necessary, page 12.

BEEF COOKING GUIDE

ITEM	TOTAL COOKING TIME	INTERNAL TEMP.*	POWER LEVEL(S)	METHOD
Roast, boneless under 4 lbs.	Rare: 7 to 10 min./lb. Med: 8 to 11 min./lb. Well: 9 to 12 min./lb.	120°F 135°F 150°F	HIGH for first 5 min. of total time, then **5**	Place roast, fat-side down, on roasting rack. Microwave to desired temp., turning over after half the time. Cover loosely with aluminum foil. Let stand for 10 min.
over 4 lbs.	Rare: 7 to 10 min./lb. Med: 8 to 11 min./lb. Well: 9 to 12 min./lb.	120°F 135°F 150°F	HIGH for first 8 min. of total time, then **5**	Same as above.
Roast, bone-in under 4 lbs.	Rare: 7 to 10 min./lb. Med: 8 to 11 min./lb. Well: 9 to 12 min./lb.	120°F 135°F 150°F	HIGH for first 5 min. of total time, then **5**	Place roast, fat-side down, on roasting rack. Microwave to desired temp., turning over after half the time. Cover loosely with aluminum foil. Let stand for 10 min.
over 4 lbs.	Rare: 7 to 10 min./lb. Med: 8 to 11 min./lb. Well: 9 to 12 min./lb.	120°F 135°F 150°F	HIGH for first 8 min. of total time, then **5**	Same as above.
Chuck Roast	30 to 35 min./lb.		**5**	Place roast in baking dish or 3-quart casserole. Add ¼ cup desired liquid and seasonings. Cover. Microwave, turning over after half the time. Let stand for 10 min.

Hamburger Patties, ¼ lb. each, ½ inch thick
  2 patties
  4 patties
	
	2 to 3 min.
	3½ to 4½ min.
			
			HIGH
				Arrange patties on roasting rack. Microwave to desired doneness, turning over after half the time. Let stand for 1 to 2 min.

*****Use temperature probe, if desired.**

HOW TO DETERMINE INTERNAL TEMPERATURE OF MEATS

USE a temperature probe or microwave thermometer to determine when large cuts of meat reach desired doneness. A probe shuts the oven off automatically when the meat reaches a pre-set temperature.

INSERT the probe or thermometer into the thickest portion of meat, making sure it does not touch gristle or bone. Do not use a probe for determining the internal temperature of poultry.

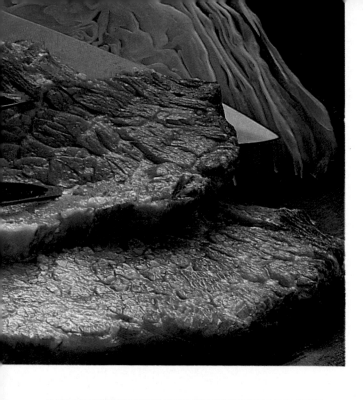

◁

CORNED BEEF AND CABBAGE

Power Levels / HIGH, **5**
Approx. Cooking Time / 1 hour 55 minutes
Yield / 8 to 10 servings

3 to 4-lb. corned beef brisket with seasoning packet
1 medium onion, sliced
1 cup water
1 head cabbage (about 1½ lbs.), cut into 8 wedges

1 In 3-quart casserole, combine brisket, contents of seasoning packet, onion and water. Cover. Microwave at HIGH for 10 minutes.

2 Reduce to POWER LEVEL **5**. Microwave for 1 to 1¼ hours longer, turning brisket over after half the time.

3 Add cabbage wedges. Re-cover. Microwave at POWER LEVEL **5** for about 30 minutes, or until brisket and cabbage wedges are tender. Let stand for 10 minutes. Slice brisket thinly across the grain. Serve with cabbage.

MARINATED SIRLOIN TIP ROAST

Power Levels / HIGH, **5**
Approx. Cooking Time / 1 hour 50 minutes
Yield / 8 to 10 servings

3 to 3½-lb. beef sirloin tip roast
½ cup Russian salad dressing
½ cup water

1 Pierce roast thoroughly with fork. Place in large plastic food storage bag. Pour Russian dressing over roast. Close bag. Refrigerate for 8 hours or overnight, turning bag over 1 or 2 times.

2 Transfer roast and dressing to 3-quart casserole. Add water. Cover. Microwave at HIGH for 5 minutes.

3 Reduce to POWER LEVEL **5**. Microwave for 1½ to 1¾ hours longer, or until roast is tender, turning over after half the time. Let stand for 10 minutes. Slice thinly across the grain.

ITALIAN MARINATED ROAST

Follow recipe above, substituting Italian salad dressing for Russian salad dressing.

ORANGE BRAISED ROAST

Power Levels / HIGH, **5**
Approx. Cooking Time / 1 hour 38 minutes
Yield / 6 to 8 servings

2½ to 3-lb. beef chuck roast
½ cup orange juice
2 tablespoons barbecue sauce or ketchup
2 tablespoons instant minced onion
1 teaspoon grated orange peel
¼ cup water
2 tablespoons cornstarch
1 can (4 oz.) sliced mushrooms, drained
1 orange, sliced
½ teaspoon salt
¼ teaspoon pepper

1 Place roast in 3-quart casserole. In small bowl, blend orange juice, barbecue sauce, onion and orange peel. Pour over roast. Cover. Microwave at HIGH for 5 minutes.

2 Reduce to POWER LEVEL **5**. Microwave for 1¼ to 1½ hours longer, or until roast is tender, turning over after half the time. Transfer roast to serving platter, reserving cooking liquid. Cover roast loosely with aluminum foil. Let stand for 10 minutes.

3 Meanwhile, in small bowl, blend water and cornstarch. Stir into cooking liquid. Add remaining ingredients. Microwave at HIGH for 2 to 3 minutes, or until mixture thickens and bubbles, stirring after every minute. Serve with roast.

OLD-FASHIONED POT ROAST ▷

Power Levels / HIGH, **5**
Approx. Cooking Time / 1 hour 50 minutes
Yield / 6 to 8 servings

2½ to 3-lb. beef chuck roast
 1 can (16 oz.) whole tomatoes, undrained
 1 medium onion, sliced and separated into rings
 ¼ teaspoon garlic powder
 ⅛ teaspoon cayenne
 ⅛ teaspoon pepper
 1 stick cinnamon
 2 medium white potatoes, quartered
 4 medium carrots, cut into 2-inch pieces
 2 stalks celery, cut into 2-inch pieces

1 Place roast in 3-quart casserole. In small bowl,
 mix tomatoes, onion, garlic powder, cayenne
 and pepper. Add cinnamon stick. Pour over
 roast. Cover. Microwave at HIGH for 5 minutes.

2 Reduce to POWER LEVEL **5**. Microwave for
 1 hour longer, turning roast over after half the
 time. Add remaining ingredients. Re-cover.
 Microwave at POWER LEVEL **5** for 30 to 45
 minutes, or until roast and vegetables are
 tender. Let stand for 10 minutes.

BRAISED BEEF BRISKET

Power Levels / HIGH, **5**
Approx. Cooking Time / 1 hour 50 minutes
Yield / 6 to 8 servings

 2 to 2½-lb. beef brisket
 1 envelope (1⅜ oz.) onion soup mix
 1 cup water

1 Place brisket in oven cooking bag. Sprinkle
 with soup mix. Add water. Tie bag loosely
 with string or nylon closure. Place in baking
 dish. Microwave at HIGH for 5 minutes.

2 Reduce to POWER LEVEL **5**. Microwave for
 1¼ to 1¾ hours longer, or until brisket is
 tender, turning bag over 1 or 2 times. Let stand
 for 10 minutes. Thinly slice, shred or chop for
 use in sandwiches and casseroles.

BARBECUED BEEF SHORT RIBS ▽

Power Levels / **7**, **3**
Approx. Cooking Time / 1 hour 45 minutes
Yield / 4 servings

3½ to 4 lbs. beef short ribs
1 small onion, thinly sliced
½ cup sliced celery
1 cup ketchup
½ cup packed brown sugar
½ cup cider vinegar
1 tablespoon Worcestershire sauce
½ teaspoon salt
¼ teaspoon dry mustard

1 Arrange ribs in 12 x 8-inch baking dish. Add onion and celery. In small mixing bowl, blend remaining ingredients. Pour over ribs. Cover dish with plastic wrap. Microwave at POWER LEVEL **7** for 15 minutes.

2 Reduce to POWER LEVEL **3**. Microwave for 1¼ to 1½ hours longer, or until ribs are tender, rearranging, turning over and basting with sauce 1 or 2 times. Let stand for 5 to 10 minutes.

STUFFED BEEF ROLLS

Power Levels / HIGH, **5**
Approx. Cooking Time / 41 minutes
Yield / 4 servings

1 to 1½-lb. beef top round steak, 1 inch thick
1½ cups chopped fresh mushrooms
¼ cup chopped onion
2 tablespoons butter or margarine
¾ cup crushed herb-seasoned stuffing mix
2 teaspoons dried parsley flakes
2 tablespoons butter or margarine
2 tablespoons cornstarch
1¼ cups water
2 teaspoons instant beef bouillon granules
½ teaspoon instant minced onion
½ teaspoon dried parsley flakes
⅛ teaspoon dried marjoram leaves

1 Cut steak in half horizontally to yield two ½-inch thick pieces. Cut each piece in half crosswise to yield total of 4 pieces. Pound each to about ¼-inch thickness. Set aside.

2 In medium mixing bowl, combine mushrooms, onion and 2 tablespoons butter. Microwave at HIGH for 4 to 5 minutes, or until onion is tender-crisp. Stir in stuffing mix and 2 teaspoons parsley flakes. Spread an equal amount of stuffing mixture on each piece of beef. Starting at shorter end, roll up jelly roll-style. Tie each roll with string to secure. Arrange rolls, seam-side down, in 9-inch square baking dish. Set aside.

3 Place 2 tablespoons butter in small mixing bowl. Microwave at HIGH for 45 to 60 seconds, or until butter melts.

4 Blend in cornstarch. Stir in remaining ingredients. Microwave at HIGH for 4½ to 5 minutes, or until mixture thickens, stirring once. Pour over beef rolls.

5 Cover dish with plastic wrap. Microwave at POWER LEVEL **5** for 25 to 30 minutes, or until beef is tender, rearranging, turning over and basting rolls with sauce 1 or 2 times. Let stand for 5 minutes.

EASY STUFFED BEEF ROLLS

Follow recipe above, substituting 1 jar (10 oz.) brown gravy for last 7 ingredients. Omit steps 3 and 4. Pour gravy over beef rolls. Continue as directed in step 5 above.

BEEF BOURGUIGNON △

Power Level / **7**
Approx. Cooking Time / 1 hour 28 minutes
Yield / 4 to 6 servings

1½ lbs. beef round steak, cut into ¾-inch cubes
2 tablespoons butter or margarine
1 can (14½ oz.) beef broth, divided
½ cup Burgundy wine
3 tablespoons brandy
2 bay leaves
⅛ teaspoon pepper
5 tablespoons all-purpose flour
1 jar (16 oz.) whole boiled onions, drained
1 cup sliced fresh mushrooms

1 In 2-quart casserole, combine beef and butter.
   Microwave at POWER LEVEL **7** for 10 to 12
   minutes, or until beef is no longer pink,
   stirring 1 or 2 times.

2 Stir in 1 cup broth, the wine, brandy, bay
   leaves and pepper. Cover. Microwave at
   POWER LEVEL **7** for about 1 hour, or until
   beef is tender, stirring 2 or 3 times.

3 In small bowl, blend remaining broth and the
   flour. Stir into beef mixture. Stir in onions and
   mushrooms. Re-cover. Microwave at POWER
   LEVEL **7** for 14 to 16 minutes, or until
   mushrooms are tender and sauce thickens,
   stirring 2 times. Let stand for 10 minutes.
   Remove and discard bay leaves.

BEEF RAGOUT

Power Levels / HIGH, **5**
Approx. Cooking Time / 1 hour 37 minutes
Yield / 6 to 8 servings

2 slices bacon, chopped
¼ cup all-purpose flour
⅛ teaspoon pepper
1 to 1½ lbs. beef round steak, about ½ inch thick,
   cut into 1½ x 1-inch pieces
1 medium onion, cut into 8 wedges
1 medium white potato, cut into ½-inch cubes
1½ cups water
1 can (7½ oz.) whole tomatoes, undrained
2 teaspoons instant beef bouillon granules
½ teaspoon dried marjoram leaves
1 bay leaf
¼ teaspoon dried thyme leaves
⅛ teaspoon pepper
   Hot cooked noodles or rice, page 122

1 Place bacon in 3-quart casserole. Microwave at
   HIGH for 2 minutes, or until crisp. Set aside.

2 In large plastic food storage bag, combine flour
   and pepper. Add beef. Shake to coat. Add beef
   and any remaining flour mixture to bacon and
   drippings. Stir in remaining ingredients except
   noodles. Cover. Microwave at HIGH for
   5 minutes.

3 Reduce to POWER LEVEL **5**. Microwave for
   1¼ to 1½ hours longer, or until beef is tender,
   stirring 1 or 2 times. Let stand for 10 minutes.
   Remove and discard bay leaf. Serve ragout
   with noodles.

BEEF STROGANOFF ▽

Power Levels / HIGH, **7**
Approx. Cooking Time / 17 minutes
Yield / 4 servings

1 medium onion, thinly sliced
3 tablespoons butter or margarine
3 tablespoons all-purpose flour
½ teaspoon salt
¼ teaspoon pepper
1 cup sliced fresh mushrooms
¾ cup beef broth
¼ teaspoon bouquet sauce
1 lb. boneless beef sirloin steak, cut into thin strips
½ cup dairy sour cream
   Hot cooked egg noodles, page 122

1 In 2-quart casserole, combine onion and butter. Microwave at HIGH for 2½ to 3½ minutes, or until onion is tender, stirring once.

2 Blend in flour, salt and pepper. Stir in mushrooms, broth and bouquet sauce. Microwave at HIGH for 3 to 4 minutes, or until mixture begins to thicken, stirring 1 or 2 times.

3 Stir in beef. Cover. Microwave at POWER LEVEL **7** for 7 to 9 minutes, or until beef is no longer pink, stirring every 2 minutes. Blend in sour cream. Microwave at POWER LEVEL **7** for 1 minute, or until heated through. Serve with egg noodles.

ORIENTAL BEEF AND BROCCOLI ▷

Power Levels / HIGH, **8**
Approx. Cooking Time / 11 minutes
Yield / 4 to 6 servings

1 tablespoon soy sauce
1 tablespoon sherry
1 clove garlic, minced
⅛ teaspoon ground ginger
1 lb. boneless beef sirloin steak, cut into thin strips
1 tablespoon vegetable oil
½ cup water
1 tablespoon soy sauce
1 tablespoon sherry
1 tablespoon cornstarch
3 cups broccoli flowerets
Sesame seed (optional)
Hot cooked rice, page 122

1 In small mixing bowl, blend 1 tablespoon soy
sauce, 1 tablespoon sherry, the garlic and
ginger. Add beef. Stir to coat. Marinate for
10 minutes.

2 Place oil in 1½-quart casserole. Microwave at
HIGH for 1 minute. Add beef mixture.
Microwave at POWER LEVEL **8** for 3 to 3½
minutes, or until beef is no longer pink,
stirring once. Remove beef with slotted spoon,
reserving cooking liquid.

3 In small mixing bowl, blend water, 1 tablespoon soy sauce, 1 tablespoon sherry and the
cornstarch. Stir into cooking liquid. Stir in
broccoli. Cover. Microwave at HIGH for 5 to 6
minutes, or until liquid thickens and broccoli
is tender, stirring once.

4 Stir in beef. Microwave, uncovered, at POWER
LEVEL **8** for 30 seconds, or until heated
through. Sprinkle with sesame seed. Serve
with rice.

TIP ▪ Beef is easier to cut into thin strips when
partially frozen. Freeze sirloin steak for about
1 hour before cutting.

CHILI ▽

Power Levels / HIGH, **8**
Approx. Cooking Time / 20 minutes
Yield / 6 to 8 servings

  1 lb. ground beef
  1 medium onion, chopped
  1 clove garlic, minced
  1 can (16 oz.) whole tomatoes, undrained
  1 can (16 oz.) kidney beans, drained
  1 can (8 oz.) tomato sauce
  1 can (4 oz.) chopped green chilies
  2 teaspoons chili powder
½ teaspoon salt
¼ teaspoon ground cumin
⅛ teaspoon ground oregano

1 In 2-quart casserole, combine ground beef, onion and garlic. Microwave at HIGH for 4 to 5 minutes, or until beef is no longer pink, stirring once. Drain.

2 Add remaining ingredients. Stir to blend and break apart tomatoes. Cover. Microwave at POWER LEVEL **8** for 10 minutes. Stir. Microwave, uncovered, at POWER LEVEL **8** for 5 minutes longer.

TEXAS CHILI

Follow recipe above, substituting 1 can (4 oz.) chopped jalapeño peppers, drained, for chilies.

BEEF STEW

Power Levels / HIGH, **5**
Approx. Cooking Time / 1 hour 35 minutes
Yield / 6 to 8 servings

½ cup all-purpose flour
  1 teaspoon salt
½ teaspoon dried thyme leaves
¼ teaspoon dried marjoram leaves
¼ teaspoon pepper
1½ to 2 lbs. beef chuck, cut into ¾-inch cubes
  3 cups beer or beef broth
  1 large onion, cut into 8 wedges
  2 stalks celery, sliced
  2 carrots, sliced
  1 can (6 oz.) tomato paste
¼ cup snipped fresh parsley
  1 teaspoon instant beef bouillon granules

1 In large plastic food storage bag, combine flour, salt, thyme, marjoram and pepper. Add beef. Shake to coat. Transfer beef and any remaining flour mixture to 5-quart casserole. Stir in remaining ingredients. Cover. Microwave at HIGH for 5 minutes.

2 Reduce to POWER LEVEL **5**. Microwave for 1¼ to 1½ hours longer, or until beef is tender, stirring every 30 minutes. Let stand for 10 minutes.

SAVORY CABBAGE ROLLS ▷

Power Level / HIGH
Approx. Cooking Time / 20 minutes
Yield / 4 servings

1 large head cabbage, cored and rinsed
1 lb. ground beef
¾ cup chopped onion
1 can (15 oz.) tomato sauce, divided
½ cup cooked white rice
¾ teaspoon salt
¼ teaspoon pepper
⅛ teaspoon dried oregano leaves
2 teaspoons packed brown sugar
¼ teaspoon dried marjoram leaves
¼ teaspoon dried oregano leaves

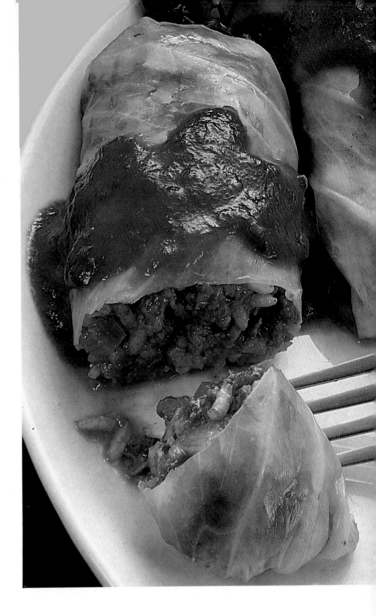

1 Place cabbage, cored-side down, in medium mixing bowl. Cover bowl with plastic wrap. Microwave at HIGH for 4 to 5 minutes, or until outer leaves are pliable. Let stand for 5 minutes. Remove 8 large leaves. Refrigerate remaining cabbage for use in other recipes.

2 In 1½-quart casserole, combine ground beef and onion. Microwave at HIGH for 4 to 5 minutes, or until beef is no longer pink, stirring once. Drain. Add ⅔ cup tomato sauce, the rice, salt, pepper and ⅛ teaspoon oregano. Mix well.

3 Continue according to photo directions below.

HOW TO ASSEMBLE AND MICROWAVE SAVORY CABBAGE ROLLS

PLACE about ⅓ cup beef mixture in center of 1 cabbage leaf. Fold opposite edges of leaf over beef mixture; roll up. Repeat with remaining beef mixture and cabbage leaves.

ARRANGE rolls, seam-side down, in 9-inch square baking dish. In small mixing bowl, blend remaining tomato sauce and remaining ingredients. Pour over cabbage rolls.

COVER dish with plastic wrap. Microwave at HIGH for 8 to 10 minutes, or until heated through and cabbage is tender, rotating dish once. Let stand for 5 minutes.

GOULASH ▽

Power Levels / HIGH, **8**
Approx. Cooking Time / 24 minutes
Yield / 4 to 6 servings

　1 lb. ground beef
　½ cup chopped onion
　½ cup thinly-sliced celery
　1 clove garlic, minced
　1 can (16 oz.) whole tomatoes, undrained
　2 teaspoons paprika
　½ teaspoon salt
　½ teaspoon sugar
　¼ teaspoon dried oregano leaves
　⅛ teaspoon caraway seed
　　Dash cayenne
　1 pkg. (7 oz.) elbow macaroni, cooked, page 122

1　In 2-quart casserole, combine ground beef, onion, celery and garlic. Microwave at HIGH for 4 to 5 minutes, or until beef is no longer pink, stirring once. Drain.

2　Add remaining ingredients except macaroni. Stir to blend and break apart tomatoes. Cover. Microwave at POWER LEVEL **8** for 14 to 16 minutes, or until celery is tender and flavors are blended.

3　Stir in macaroni. Re-cover. Microwave at POWER LEVEL **8** for 2 to 3 minutes, or until heated through.

SWEDISH MEATBALLS

Power Levels / **9**, **7**
Approx. Cooking Time / 13 minutes
Yield / 4 to 6 servings

　1 lb. ground beef
　½ cup unseasoned dry bread crumbs
　½ cup milk*
　¼ cup finely-chopped onion
　1 egg, slightly beaten
　2 teaspoons dried parsley flakes
　½ teaspoon salt
　½ teaspoon ground nutmeg
　¼ teaspoon ground allspice
　¼ teaspoon pepper
　1 tablespoon all-purpose flour
　　Dash salt
　½ cup half-and-half

1　In medium mixing bowl, combine ground beef, bread crumbs, milk, onion, egg, parsley flakes, ½ teaspoon salt, the nutmeg, allspice and pepper. Mix well. Shape into 1½ to 2-inch balls. Arrange in 12 x 8-inch baking dish.

2　Microwave at POWER LEVEL **9** for 7 to 9 minutes, or until meatballs are firm and no longer pink, rearranging and turning over 1 or 2 times. Remove meatballs with slotted spoon, reserving drippings. Set aside.

3　Blend flour and dash salt into drippings. Stir in half-and-half. Microwave at POWER LEVEL **7** for 3 to 3½ minutes, or until mixture slightly thickens, stirring 1 or 2 times. Add meatballs. Stir to coat. Microwave at POWER LEVEL **7** for 1 minute, or until hot.

*For firmer meatballs, reduce milk to ⅓ cup.

STUFFED GREEN PEPPERS ▷

Power Level / HIGH
Approx. Cooking Time / 20 minutes
Yield / 4 servings

FILLING
1 lb. ground beef
⅓ cup finely-chopped onion
1 can (8 oz.) tomato sauce
¼ cup water
1 tablespoon grated Parmesan cheese
¾ teaspoon salt
¼ teaspoon dried marjoram leaves
⅛ teaspoon pepper
½ cup uncooked instant rice

4 medium green peppers

SAUCE
1 can (8 oz.) tomato sauce
2 teaspoons packed brown sugar
¼ teaspoon dried marjoram leaves
⅛ teaspoon pepper

2 tablespoons grated Parmesan cheese

1 For filling, in 1-quart casserole, combine
   ground beef and onion. Microwave at HIGH
   for 4 to 5 minutes, or until beef is no longer
   pink, stirring once. Drain. Stir in tomato
   sauce, water, Parmesan cheese, salt, marjoram
   and pepper. Cover.

2 Microwave at HIGH for 2½ to 3½ minutes, or
   until mixture bubbles. Stir in rice. Re-cover.
   Let stand for 5 minutes. Continue according to
   photo directions below.

HOW TO ASSEMBLE AND MICROWAVE STUFFED GREEN PEPPERS

CUT green peppers in half
lengthwise. Remove seeds and
stems. Arrange pepper halves,
cut-side up, in 12 x 8-inch
baking dish.

SPOON an equal amount of
filling into each pepper half. For
sauce, in small bowl, blend all
ingredients. Pour over peppers.
Sprinkle with Parmesan cheese.

COVER dish with plastic wrap.
Microwave at HIGH for 10 to 12
minutes, or until peppers are
tender, rotating dish once. Let
stand for 5 minutes.

PORCUPINE MEATBALLS △

Power Levels / HIGH, **7**
Approx. Cooking Time / 18 minutes
Yield / 4 to 6 servings

 2 slices bacon, chopped
 2 tablespoons finely-chopped green pepper
 2 tablespoons finely-chopped onion
 1 lb. ground beef
 ¾ cup uncooked instant rice
 ¼ cup milk
 1 egg, slightly beaten
 ½ teaspoon salt
 ¼ teaspoon pepper
 1 can (10¾ oz.) condensed cream of mushroom soup
 3 tablespoons red wine or water
 1 teaspoon dried parsley flakes
 ⅛ teaspoon dried thyme leaves

1 In medium mixing bowl, combine bacon,
   green pepper and onion. Microwave at HIGH
   for 2½ to 3½ minutes, or until bacon is brown,
   stirring once.

2 Add ground beef, rice, milk, egg, salt and
   pepper. Mix well. Shape into 1½-inch balls.
   Arrange in 12 x 8-inch baking dish.

3 In small mixing bowl, blend remaining ingredients. Pour over meatballs. Cover dish with
   plastic wrap. Microwave at POWER LEVEL **7**
   for 13 to 15 minutes, or until meatballs are firm
   and no longer pink, rearranging and turning
   over 2 times. Let stand for 3 minutes.

EASY SALISBURY STEAK

Power Level / **9**
Approx. Cooking Time / 18 minutes
Yield / 6 servings

1½ lbs. ground beef
 1 can (10¾ oz.) condensed cream of mushroom
    soup, divided
 1 can (4 oz.) sliced mushrooms, drained, divided
 ½ cup milk
 ½ cup unseasoned dry bread crumbs
 1 egg, slightly beaten
 ¼ cup finely-chopped onion
 ⅛ teaspoon pepper
 ½ cup milk
 2 teaspoons dried parsley flakes

1 In large mixing bowl, combine ground beef,
   ⅓ cup soup, ½ cup mushrooms, ½ cup milk,
   the bread crumbs, egg, onion and pepper.
   Mix well. Shape into six 1-inch thick patties.

2 Arrange patties in 12 x 8-inch baking dish.
   Cover dish with wax paper. Microwave at
   POWER LEVEL **9** for 10 to 12 minutes, or
   until patties are no longer pink, rearranging
   and turning over after half the time. Drain.

3 In small bowl, combine remaining soup,
   remaining mushrooms, ½ cup milk and the
   parsley flakes. Pour over patties. Re-cover.
   Microwave at POWER LEVEL **9** for 5 to 6
   minutes, or until heated through.

HAMBURGER PIE ▹

Power Levels / HIGH, 7
Approx. Cooking Time / 19 minutes
Yield / 4 to 6 servings

1 pkg. (10 oz.) frozen mixed vegetables
1 lb. ground beef
¼ cup chopped green onion
½ cup milk
½ cup instant mashed potato flakes
1 egg, slightly beaten
¼ cup ketchup
1 teaspoon dried parsley flakes
½ teaspoon dried basil leaves
½ teaspoon garlic salt
¼ teaspoon pepper
1 frozen deep dish pie crust, microwaved, page 134*
4 servings instant mashed potatoes
1 cup shredded Cheddar cheese (about 4 oz.)

1 Remove vegetables from packaging and place on plate. Microwave at HIGH for 2½ to 3 minutes. Let stand for 5 minutes. Set aside.

2 In 2-quart casserole, combine ground beef and onion. Microwave at HIGH for 4 to 5 minutes, or until beef is no longer pink, stirring once. Drain. Add vegetables, milk, potato flakes, egg, ketchup, parsley flakes, basil, garlic salt and pepper. Mix well. Spread evenly in pie crust.

3 Prepare mashed potatoes according to package directions. Mound onto top of pie, or use pastry tube to pipe onto pie. Sprinkle with Cheddar cheese.

4 Microwave at POWER LEVEL 7 for 9 to 11 minutes, or until heated through and cheese melts, rotating pie plate after half the time. Let stand for 5 minutes.

***Prepare and microwave 1 recipe Single Pie Crust (page 141) and substitute for frozen pie crust, if desired.**

MINI MEATLOAF

Power Level / 7
Approx. Cooking Time / 20 minutes
Yield / 4 servings

1 lb. ground beef
⅓ cup unseasoned dry bread crumbs
¼ cup ketchup
1 egg, slightly beaten
1 tablespoon milk
2 teaspoons instant minced onion
½ teaspoon salt
⅛ teaspoon pepper
⅛ teaspoon garlic powder

1 In medium mixing bowl, combine all ingredients. Mix well. Shape into 6 x 4-inch loaf. Place in 8 x 4-inch loaf dish.

2 Microwave at POWER LEVEL 7 for 15 to 20 minutes, or until beef is no longer pink and internal temperature registers 150°F,* rotating dish once. Cover loosely with aluminum foil. Let stand for 5 minutes. Remove from dish.

***Use temperature probe, if desired.**

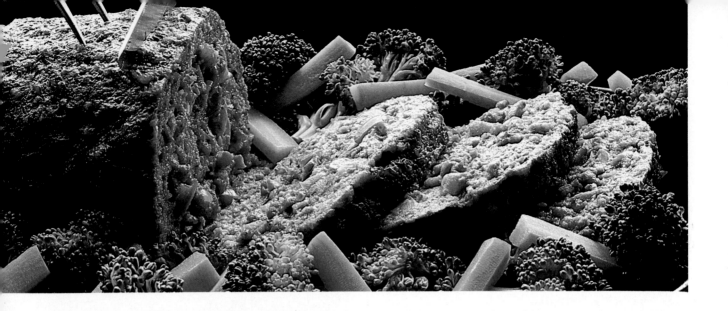

ROLLED ITALIAN MEATLOAF △

Power Levels / HIGH, **6**
Approx. Cooking Time / 38 minutes
Yield / 6 to 8 servings

LOAF

1½ lbs. ground beef
2 eggs, slightly beaten
⅓ cup milk
6 tablespoons quick-cooking rolled oats
¾ teaspoon salt
½ teaspoon Worcestershire sauce
½ teaspoon Italian seasoning
¼ teaspoon pepper
⅛ teaspoon garlic powder

FILLING

½ lb. bulk Italian sausage
¾ cup chopped green pepper
2 tablespoons finely-chopped onion
3 tablespoons capers or chopped green olives
2 tablespoons seasoned dry bread crumbs

1 For loaf, in medium mixing bowl, combine all ingredients. Mix well. On sheet of wax paper, pat mixture into 14 x 9-inch rectangle.

2 For filling, in 1-quart casserole, combine sausage, green pepper and onion. Microwave at HIGH for 2½ to 3 minutes, or until sausage is no longer pink, stirring once. Drain. Stir in capers and bread crumbs.

3 Assemble meatloaf according to photo directions below.

4 Microwave at POWER LEVEL **6** for 30 to 35 minutes, or until no longer pink and internal temperature registers 150°F,* rotating dish 2 times. Cover loosely with aluminum foil. Let stand for 5 minutes. Remove from dish.

*Use temperature probe, if desired.

HOW TO ASSEMBLE MEATLOAF

SPREAD filling evenly over loaf mixture, leaving a 1-inch border on all sides.

ROLL UP jelly roll-style, starting with shorter side, using wax paper to lift and roll. Press ends and seam to seal.

PLACE seam-side down in 8 x 4-inch loaf dish. Microwave as directed in step 4 above.

LASAGNA ▷

Power Levels / HIGH, **5**
Approx. Cooking Time / 49 minutes
Yield / 8 to 10 servings

 1 lb. ground beef
½ lb. bulk Italian sausage
⅓ cup chopped onion
 1 can (16 oz.) whole tomatoes, undrained
 1 can (15 oz.) tomato sauce
½ cup water
 2 teaspoons Italian seasoning
¼ teaspoon pepper
 1 carton (15 oz.) ricotta cheese
 3 cups shredded mozzarella cheese (about 12 oz.),
   divided
 1 egg
¼ teaspoon garlic powder
 9 *uncooked* lasagna noodles

1 In 2-quart casserole, combine ground beef,
   sausage and onion. Microwave at HIGH for
   5 to 6 minutes, or until meat is no longer pink,
   stirring 2 times. Drain. Add tomatoes, tomato
   sauce, water, Italian seasoning and pepper.
   Stir to blend and break apart tomatoes.
   Set aside.

2 In medium mixing bowl, combine ricotta
   cheese, ½ cup mozzarella cheese, the egg and
   garlic powder. Mix well. Set aside.

3 Spread one-third of meat mixture in bottom of
   12 x 8-inch baking dish. Arrange 3 noodles on
   top. Spread with half the ricotta mixture.
   Sprinkle with 1 cup mozzarella cheese. Repeat
   layers once. Cover with remaining noodles.
   Top with remaining meat mixture.

4 Cover dish with plastic wrap. Microwave at
   HIGH for 8 minutes. Rotate dish. Reduce to
   POWER LEVEL **5**. Microwave for 30 to 35
   minutes longer, or until noodles are tender,
   rotating dish once. Sprinkle with remaining
   ½ cup mozzarella cheese. Re-cover. Let stand
   for 10 minutes.

PORK

· PORK DEFROSTING GUIDE

ITEM	TOTAL DEFROSTING TIME	POWER LEVEL	METHOD
Roast, boneless and bone-in	11 to 14 min./lb.	**3**	Remove packaging. Place roast on roasting rack. Microwave until wooden pick can be easily inserted in center, turning over after half the time.* Cover loosely with aluminum foil. Let stand for 15 to 20 min.
Spareribs	4 to 6 min./lb.	**5**	Remove packaging. Place ribs on roasting rack. Microwave until pliable, breaking apart and rearranging as soon as possible.* Let stand for 5 to 10 min.
Pork Chops	5 to 7 min./lb.	**5**	Remove packaging. Place chops on roasting rack. Microwave until pliable, breaking apart and rearranging as soon as possible.* Let stand for 5 to 10 min.
Stew Meat	5 to 7 min./lb.	**5**	Remove packaging. Place pork on plate. Microwave until wooden pick can be easily inserted in each piece, breaking apart and rearranging as soon as possible. Let stand for 5 to 10 min.
Ground Pork	4 to 6 min./lb.	**5**	Remove packaging. Place pork on plate. Microwave, breaking apart and removing defrosted portions as soon as possible. Let stand for 5 to 10 min.

*Shield warm areas as necessary, page 12.

PORK COOKING GUIDE

ITEM	TOTAL COOKING TIME	POWER LEVEL	INTERNAL TEMP.*	METHOD
Roast, boneless and bone-in	9 to 12 min./lb.	HIGH for first 5 min. of total time, then **5**	165°F	Place roast, fat-side down, on roasting rack. Microwave, turning roast over after half the time and rotating rack 2 times. Cover loosely with aluminum foil. Let stand for 10 min.
Ham canned 1 lb. 3 to 5 lbs.	18 to 22 min. 10 to 15 min./lb.	**5**	130°F	Remove packaging. Place ham in baking dish. Cover dish loosely with plastic wrap. Microwave, turning over after half the time. Let stand for 5 min.
rolled boneless	15 to 20 min./lb.	**5**	130°F	Same as above.
Bacon 2 slices 4 slices 8 slices	2 to 2½ min. 3½ to 4 min. 5½ to 6 min.	HIGH		Arrange bacon on roasting rack. Cover with paper towel. Microwave until crisp, turning over after half the time. Let stand for 1 min.

*Use temperature probe, if desired.

PORK LOIN ROAST WITH APRICOT GLAZE ▽

Power Levels / HIGH, **5**
Approx. Cooking Time / 51 minutes
Yield / 8 to 10 servings

½ cup water
2 tablespoons cornstarch
1 pkg. (6 oz.) dried apricots, chopped
1 cup apricot nectar or apple juice
2 tablespoons orange juice
2 tablespoons honey
1 tablespoon lemon juice
1 stick cinnamon
3 to 3½-lb. boneless pork loin roast
    Pepper

1 In small mixing bowl, blend water and
   cornstarch. Stir in apricots, apricot nectar,
   orange juice, honey, lemon juice and
   cinnamon stick. Microwave at HIGH for 5 to 6
   minutes, or until glaze thickens and becomes
   translucent, stirring 2 or 3 times. Remove and
   discard cinnamon stick. Set glaze aside.

2 Rub roast with pepper. Place roast, fat-side
   down, on roasting rack. Microwave at HIGH
   for 5 minutes.

3 Reduce to POWER LEVEL **5**. Microwave for
   30 to 40 minutes longer, or until internal
   temperature registers 165°F,* turning roast over
   and brushing with glaze after half the time,
   and rotating rack 2 times. Cover loosely with
   aluminum foil. Let stand for 10 to 15 minutes.
   Serve with remaining glaze.

*Use temperature probe, if desired.

SAVORY PORK CHOPS AND RICE

Power Levels / HIGH, **5**, **7**
Approx. Cooking Time / 41 minutes
Yield / 4 servings

1 package (6¼ oz.) quick-cooking long grain and
    wild rice
    Water and butter or margarine as directed on
    rice package
4 pork chops, ½ inch thick
4 thin slices onion
4 thin slices green pepper (rings)
1 can (16 oz.) stewed tomatoes
½ teaspoon dried marjoram leaves
½ teaspoon salt
¼ teaspoon garlic powder

1 In 2-quart casserole, combine rice, water and
   butter as directed on package. Cover. Microwave at HIGH for 5 to 6 minutes, or until
   water boils.

2 Reduce to POWER LEVEL **5**. Microwave for
   5 minutes longer. Set aside.

3 Arrange chops in 9-inch square baking dish
   with meaty portions toward outside of dish.
   Place one onion and one green pepper slice
   on each chop. In small mixing bowl, mix
   remaining ingredients. Pour over chops. Cover
   dish with wax paper. Microwave at POWER
   LEVEL **7** for 20 to 25 minutes, or until chops
   are no longer pink, rotating dish 2 times.

4 Stir rice. Arrange chops on rice. Place
   tomatoes on chops. Microwave at POWER
   LEVEL **7** for 3 to 5 minutes, or until hot.

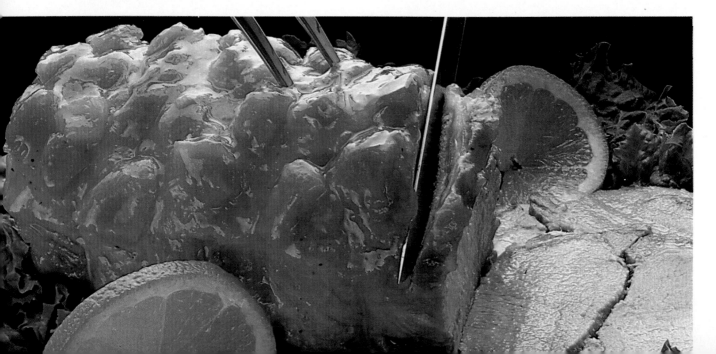

APPLE-STUFFED PORK CHOPS ▷

Power Level / **7**
Approx. Cooking Time / 18 minutes
Yield / 4 servings

 4 center-cut pork chops, ¾ to 1 inch thick
¼ teaspoon pepper
½ cup finely-chopped apple
¼ cup thinly-sliced celery
 3 tablespoons raisins
¼ teaspoon ground cinnamon
½ cup apple juice
 2 teaspoons water
½ teaspoon bouquet sauce
¼ cup apple juice
 2 tablespoons all-purpose flour
½ teaspoon salt

1 Assemble pork chops according to photo
   directions below.

2 In small bowl, blend water and bouquet sauce.
   Brush onto chops. Cover dish with wax paper.
   Microwave at POWER LEVEL **7** for 14 to 16
   minutes, or until chops are no longer pink,
   rotating dish and brushing chops with diluted
   bouquet sauce after half the time. Transfer
   chops to serving platter, reserving drippings.
   Cover chops loosely with aluminum foil.
   Let stand for 5 minutes.

3 Meanwhile, in small mixing bowl, blend ¼
   cup apple juice, the flour and salt. Stir into
   drippings. Microwave at POWER LEVEL **7**
   for about 2 minutes, or until mixture thickens,
   stirring once. Serve with chops.

HOW TO ASSEMBLE APPLE-STUFFED PORK CHOPS

CUT through each chop
horizontally to form a pocket,
leaving a 1-inch border at sides
of chop. Sprinkle dash of
pepper into each pocket.

MIX apple, celery, raisins and
cinnamon in small mixing bowl.
Stuff each chop with an equal
amount of mixture. Secure
openings with wooden picks.

ARRANGE chops in 9-inch
baking dish with meaty portions toward outside of dish.
Add ½ cup apple juice. Continue as directed in step 2 above.

SEASONED PORK CHOPS

Power Level / **7**
Approx. Cooking Time / 16 minutes
Yield / 6 servings

 6 pork chops, about ½ inch thick
 1 envelope (about 2 oz.) seasoned coating for pork

1 Coat chops with seasoned coating according
   to package directions. Arrange chops on
   roasting rack.

2 Microwave at POWER LEVEL **7** for 12½ to
   16½ minutes, or until chops are no longer
   pink, rearranging after half the time.

ORIENTAL PORK AND CABBAGE

Power Level / **8**
Approx. Cooking Time / 16 minutes
Yield / 4 to 6 servings

 3 tablespoons soy sauce
 ⅛ teaspoon garlic powder
 ⅛ teaspoon dried crushed red pepper
 1 to 1½ lbs. butterflied pork chops, cut into 1-inch
    chunks
 ¼ cup water
 1 tablespoon soy sauce
 2 teaspoons cornstarch
 1 teaspoon instant chicken bouillon granules
 2 cups coarsely-chopped cabbage
 ½ cup green onion pieces, 1-inch pieces
 ⅓ cup thinly-sliced celery
    Hot cooked rice, page 122

1 In 2-quart casserole, blend 3 tablespoons soy
   sauce, the garlic powder and red pepper.
   Add pork. Stir to coat. Marinate for 10 to 15
   minutes. Microwave at POWER LEVEL **8** for
   5 minutes, stirring 2 times.

2 In small bowl, blend water, 1 tablespoon soy
   sauce, the cornstarch and bouillon granules.
   Stir into pork mixture. Stir in cabbage, onion
   and celery. Cover. Microwave at POWER
   LEVEL **8** for 9 to 11 minutes, or until pork is
   no longer pink and cabbage is tender, stirring
   after half the time. Serve with rice.

LEMON SAGE PORK CHOPS

Power Level / **7**
Approx. Cooking Time / 13 minutes
Yield / 4 servings

 2 tablespoons vegetable oil
 1 tablespoon lemon juice
 ½ teaspoon ground sage
 ½ teaspoon dry mustard
 ¼ teaspoon pepper
 ¼ teaspoon bouquet sauce
 ⅛ teaspoon garlic powder
 4 pork chops, about ½ inch thick

1 In small bowl, blend all ingredients except
   chops. Place chops in large plastic food
   storage bag or 9-inch square baking dish.
   Pour marinade over chops. Close bag or cover
   dish. Marinate for 15 minutes, turning chops
   over once.

2 Remove chops from bag, reserving marinade.
   Arrange chops on roasting rack with meaty
   portions toward outside of rack. Microwave at
   POWER LEVEL **7** for 11 to 13 minutes, or
   until chops are no longer pink, turning over
   and basting with marinade after half the time.

SOUTHERN BARBECUED RIBS

Power Level / **5**
Approx. Cooking Time / 50 minutes
Yield / 2 or 3 servings

 2 lbs. spareribs, cut into serving-size pieces
 1 small onion, sliced
 ½ cup hot water
 1 bay leaf
 1 cup barbecue sauce
 2 tablespoons honey
 1 tablespoon soy sauce

1 In 3-quart casserole, combine ribs, onion,
   water and bay leaf. Cover. Microwave at
   POWER LEVEL **5** for 30 to 40 minutes, or
   until ribs are tender, rearranging and turning
   over after half the time. Drain. Remove and
   discard bay leaf.

2 In small mixing bowl, blend remaining
   ingredients. Pour over ribs. Microwave at
   POWER LEVEL **5** for about 10 minutes,
   or until sauce is heated through.

SWEET-AND-SOUR PORK ▷

Power Level / **7**
Approx. Cooking Time / 24 minutes
Yield / 4 to 6 servings

  1 can (8 oz.) pineapple chunks packed in juice
⅓ cup cider vinegar
⅓ cup packed brown sugar
  3 tablespoons ketchup
  3 tablespoons cornstarch
  2 tablespoons soy sauce
¼ teaspoon garlic powder
⅛ teaspoon cayenne
  1 to 1½ lbs. butterflied pork chops, cut into 1-inch chunks
  1 medium onion, cut into 1-inch pieces
  1 medium green pepper, cored, seeded and cut into thin strips
  2 medium carrots, thinly sliced
  1 medium tomato, seeded and cut into chunks
    Hot cooked rice, page 122

1 Drain pineapple juice into 2-quart casserole. Set pineapple chunks aside. Blend vinegar, brown sugar, ketchup, cornstarch, soy sauce, garlic powder and cayenne into juice. Stir in pork. Microwave at POWER LEVEL **7** for 9 to 12 minutes, or until pork is no longer pink, stirring every 3 minutes.

2 Stir in onion, green pepper and carrots. Cover. Microwave at POWER LEVEL **7** for 6 to 9 minutes, or until sauce thickens and becomes translucent, and vegetables are tender-crisp, stirring every 3 minutes.

3 Stir in tomato and pineapple chunks. Microwave, uncovered, at POWER LEVEL **7** for 2 to 3 minutes, or until heated through. Serve with rice.

HAM STEAK WITH RAISIN SAUCE △

Power Levels / HIGH, **9**
Approx. Cooking Time / 14 minutes
Yield / 4 to 6 servings

½ cup water
1 tablespoon cornstarch
⅓ cup currant jelly
⅓ cup raisins
⅓ cup orange juice
½ teaspoon grated orange peel
⅛ teaspoon ground allspice
1½ to 1¾-lb. fully-cooked ham steak, 1 inch thick

1 In small mixing bowl, blend water and cornstarch. Stir in remaining ingredients except ham. Microwave at HIGH for 3½ to 4½ minutes, or until sauce thickens and becomes translucent, stirring after every minute. Set aside.

2 Place ham in 12 x 8-inch baking dish. Cover dish with plastic wrap. Microwave at POWER LEVEL **9** for 8 to 9 minutes, or until ham is heated through, turning over after half the time.

3 Pour sauce over ham. Microwave, uncovered, at POWER LEVEL **9** for 1 minute, or until hot. Cover loosely with aluminum foil. Let stand for 2 to 3 minutes.

COUNTRY HAM CASSEROLE △

Power Levels / HIGH, **9**
Approx. Cooking Time / 20 minutes
Yield / 6 to 8 servings

1 pkg. (10 oz.) frozen cut asparagus
1 can (10¾ oz.) condensed cream of celery soup
¾ cup milk
½ teaspoon dry mustard (optional)
3 cups cooked egg noodles, page 122
2 cups cubed fully-cooked ham, ½-inch cubes
1½ cups shredded Swiss cheese (about 6 oz.), divided
1 can (3 oz.) French-fried onions, crushed

1 Remove asparagus from packaging and place on plate. Microwave at HIGH for 3 minutes. Let stand for 5 minutes.

2 In 3-quart casserole, blend soup, milk and mustard. Stir in asparagus, noodles, ham and 1¼ cups Swiss cheese. Cover. Microwave at POWER LEVEL **9** for 5 minutes. Stir.

3 Sprinkle with remaining ¼ cup Swiss cheese. Top with crushed onions. Microwave, uncovered, at POWER LEVEL **9** for 10 to 12 minutes, or until heated through and internal temperature registers 145°F.* Let stand for 3 to 5 minutes.

*Use temperature probe, if desired.

SAUSAGE AND BEAN CASSEROLE △

Power Levels / HIGH, **7**
Approx. Cooking Time / 24 minutes
Yield / 8 to 10 servings

 2 small onions, sliced
1½ lbs. smoked Polish sausage, cut into 1½-inch
    pieces
 2 cans (16 oz. each) navy or small white beans,
    rinsed and drained
½ lb. fully-cooked ham, cut into ¾-inch cubes
 1 can (8 oz.) tomato sauce
½ cup ketchup
¼ cup white wine or chicken broth
¼ cup packed brown sugar
¾ teaspoon salt
½ teaspoon dry mustard
½ teaspoon pepper

1 Place onions in 3-quart casserole. Microwave
   at HIGH for 3 to 4 minutes, or until tender,
   stirring once.

2 Stir in remaining ingredients. Cover. Microwave at HIGH for 5 minutes. Stir. Re-cover.

3 Reduce to POWER LEVEL **7**. Microwave for
   10 to 15 minutes longer, or until flavors are
   blended, stirring 2 times.

STUFFED HERB BURGERS △

Power Level / **7**
Approx. Cooking Time / 10 minutes
Yield / 4 servings

¾ lb. ground pork
¼ lb. lean ground beef
 1 teaspoon dried parsley flakes
¼ teaspoon dried dill weed
¼ teaspoon dried oregano leaves
⅛ teaspoon fennel seed
⅛ teaspoon garlic powder
⅛ teaspoon pepper
¼ cup shredded mozzarella cheese (about 1 oz.)

1 In medium mixing bowl, combine all
   ingredients except mozzarella cheese. Mix
   well. Shape into eight 3½-inch diameter
   patties. Place 1 tablespoon mozzarella cheese
   on center of each of 4 patties. Top with
   remaining patties. Press edges to seal.

2 Arrange patties on roasting rack. Microwave at
   POWER LEVEL **7** for 8½ to 10 minutes, or
   until firm and no longer pink, turning patties
   over and rotating rack after half the time.
   Let stand for 2 to 3 minutes.

HAM AND APPLE RING

Power Levels / **9**, HIGH
Approx. Cooking Time / 20 minutes
Yield / 6 to 8 servings

RING

1½ lbs. ground fully-cooked ham
1 small apple, cored, peeled and chopped
1 cup soft bread crumbs
3 eggs, slightly beaten
½ cup milk
⅓ cup finely-chopped onion
¼ cup honey
¼ teaspoon ground cloves
¼ teaspoon ground ginger
⅛ teaspoon pepper

TOPPING

4 small apples, cored, peeled and sliced
2 tablespoons butter or margarine
1 tablespoon honey

1 Prepare ring according to photo directions
  below.

2 Microwave ring at POWER LEVEL **9** for 12 to
  13 minutes, or until set, rotating pie plate after
  half the time. Cover loosely with aluminum
  foil. Set aside.

3 For topping, in small mixing bowl, combine all
  ingredients. Microwave at HIGH for 6 to 7
  minutes, or until apples are tender,
  stirring once.

4 Drain liquid from ring. Invert onto serving
  plate. Spoon topping over ring.

HOW TO PREPARE RING

COMBINE all ingredients for ring in medium
mixing bowl. Mix well. Spoon mixture around
edge of 9-inch pie plate. Form into ring, leaving
about 2½ inches open in center. Continue as
directed in step 2 above.

CHEESE AND MUSHROOM HAM LOAF

Power Level / **7**
Approx. Cooking Time / 30 minutes
Yield / 6 to 8 servings

LOAF

1 lb. ground fully-cooked ham
½ lb. ground pork
2 eggs, slightly beaten
½ cup seasoned dry bread crumbs
⅓ cup milk
¼ cup finely-chopped onion
1 tablespoon Dijon mustard
½ teaspoon dried parsley flakes
⅛ teaspoon pepper
⅛ teaspoon ground nutmeg

FILLING

½ cup shredded Swiss cheese (about 2 oz.)
½ cup chopped fresh mushrooms

TOPPING

1 tablespoon Dijon mustard
1 tablespoon light corn syrup
Dash pepper

1 For loaf, in medium mixing bowl, combine all
  ingredients. Mix well. Press half of mixture
  into bottom and about 1 inch up sides of
  9 x 5-inch loaf dish. Sprinkle with filling
  ingredients, leaving a ½-inch border on all
  sides. Spread remaining loaf mixture over
  filling, pressing edges to seal.

2 For topping, in small bowl, blend all
  ingredients. Spread on loaf. Microwave at
  POWER LEVEL **7** for 25 to 30 minutes, or
  until loaf is set and internal temperature
  registers 165°F,* rotating dish 2 times. Cover
  loosely with aluminum foil. Let stand for
  5 to 10 minutes.

*Use temperature probe, if desired.

ITALIAN MEATBALLS AND TOMATO SAUCE △

Power Level / HIGH
Approx. Cooking Time / 27 minutes
Yield / 4 to 6 servings

MEATBALLS

1 lb. bulk Italian sausage
½ lb. ground beef
⅓ cup seasoned dry bread crumbs
¼ cup finely-chopped onion
1 egg, slightly beaten
2 tablespoons snipped fresh parsley
2 tablespoons milk
1 tablespoon grated Parmesan cheese
¼ teaspoon salt
⅛ teaspoon pepper

2 cans (16 oz. each) tomato sauce
1 can (6 oz.) tomato paste
2 tablespoons sugar
2 teaspoons Italian seasoning
¼ teaspoon garlic powder
1 cup sliced fresh mushrooms
  Hot cooked spaghetti, page 122

1 For meatballs, in medium mixing bowl, combine all ingredients. Mix well. Shape into 1½ to 2-inch balls. Arrange in 3-quart casserole. Microwave at HIGH for 7 to 9 minutes, or until meatballs are no longer pink on the outside, rearranging and turning over once. Drain. Set aside.

2 In 2-quart casserole, blend tomato sauce, tomato paste, sugar, Italian seasoning and garlic powder. Microwave at HIGH for 9 to 10 minutes, or until flavors are blended. Stir in mushrooms.

3 Pour sauce over meatballs. Cover. Microwave at HIGH for 6 to 8 minutes, or until mushrooms are tender and meatballs are firm and cooked through. Serve with spaghetti.

SAUSAGE COOKING GUIDE

ITEM	TOTAL COOKING TIME	POWER LEVEL	METHOD
Polish Sausage, Bratwurst or other large sausage			
fully cooked			
1 sausage	1 to 1½ min.	HIGH	Pierce each sausage 1 or 2 times with fork. Arrange on roasting rack. Microwave until hot, turning over and rearranging after half the time.
2 sausages	1¾ to 2½ min.		
4 sausages	3 to 4 min.		
fresh (uncooked)			
1 sausage	1¼ to 1½ min.	HIGH	Pierce each sausage 1 or 2 times with fork. Arrange on roasting rack. Microwave until firm and no longer pink, turning over and rearranging after half the time.
2 sausages	3 to 3½ min.		
4 sausages	5 to 6 min.		
Wieners			
1	30 to 45 sec.	HIGH	Pierce each wiener 1 or 2 times with fork. Arrange on roasting rack. Microwave until hot, rotating rack after half the time.
2	45 to 60 sec.		
4	1¼ to 1¾ min.		
Links			
fully cooked			
2 links	30 to 60 sec.	HIGH	Arrange links on roasting rack. Microwave until hot. Let stand for 1 min.
4 links	1 to 1½ min.		
8 links	1½ to 2 min.		
fresh (uncooked)			
2 links	1 to 2 min.	HIGH	Pierce each link 1 or 2 times with fork. Arrange on roasting rack. Microwave until firm and no longer pink, turning over and rearranging after half the time. Let stand for 1 to 2 min.
4 links	1½ to 2½ min.		
8 links	2½ to 3½ min.		
Patties			
fully cooked			
2 patties	30 to 60 sec.	HIGH	Arrange patties on roasting rack. Microwave until hot. Let stand for 1 min.
4 patties	1 to 1½ min.		
8 patties	1½ to 2 min.		
fresh (uncooked), ½ inch thick			
2 patties	2 to 2½ min.	HIGH	Arrange patties on roasting rack. Microwave until firm and no longer pink, turning over after half the time. Let stand for 2 to 3 min.
4 patties	3 to 3½ min.		
8 patties	5 to 5½ min.		

SAUSAGE WITH SWEET-AND-SOUR CABBAGE

Power Level / HIGH
Approx. Cooking Time / 20 minutes
Yield / 4 to 6 servings

  1 head red cabbage (1½ to 2 lbs.), coarsely chopped
  1 medium apple, cored and chopped
  ¼ cup sugar
  ¼ cup cider vinegar
  2 to 3 teaspoons instant minced onion
  ½ teaspoon caraway seed
  ½ teaspoon salt
  1 to 1½-lb. Polish sausage ring

1 In 12 x 8-inch baking dish, combine all ingredients except Polish sausage. Mix well. Cover dish with plastic wrap. Microwave at HIGH for 7 minutes. Stir.

2 Slash sausage at 3 to 4-inch intervals. Place on cabbage mixture. Re-cover. Microwave at HIGH for 12 to 13 minutes, or until sausage is heated through and cabbage is tender-crisp. Let stand for 5 minutes.

SAUSAGE STEW

Power Levels / HIGH, **5**
Approx. Cooking Time / 1 hour
Yield / 6 to 8 servings

  1 can (28 oz.) whole tomatoes, undrained, cut up
  1 lb. boneless pork stew meat, cut into ¾-inch cubes
  1 lb. fresh (uncooked) sausage links, cut in half
  1 can (8 oz.) tomato sauce
  1 large green pepper, cored, seeded and cut into 1-inch pieces
  1 teaspoon dried basil leaves
  1 teaspoon dried oregano leaves
  1 teaspoon sugar
  ¼ teaspoon garlic powder
  Hot cooked rice or pasta, page 122 (optional)

1 In 3-quart casserole, combine all ingredients except rice. Mix well. Cover. Microwave at HIGH for 5 minutes.

2 Reduce to POWER LEVEL **5**. Microwave for 45 to 55 minutes longer, or until pork is tender, stirring occasionally. Skim grease from surface. Serve with rice.

QUICK BOLOGNA AND SAUERKRAUT ▽

Power Levels / HIGH, **8**
Approx. Cooking Time / 13 minutes
Yield / 4 servings

  ¼ cup chopped green pepper
  2 tablespoons chopped green onion
  1 jar (16 oz.) sauerkraut, drained
  1 jar (2 oz.) sliced pimiento, drained
  1 tablespoon packed brown sugar
  ⅛ teaspoon pepper
  1-lb. fully-cooked bologna ring

1 In 9-inch square baking dish, combine green pepper and onion. Microwave at HIGH for 2 minutes, or until tender-crisp.

2 Stir in remaining ingredients except bologna. Slash bologna at 3-inch intervals. Place on top of sauerkraut mixture. Microwave at POWER LEVEL **8** for 10 to 11 minutes, or until heated through, rotating dish after half the time. Cover loosely with aluminum foil. Let stand for 3 to 4 minutes.

LAMB

LAMB DEFROSTING GUIDE

ITEM	TOTAL DEFROSTING TIME	POWER LEVEL	METHOD
Roast boneless	9 to 12 min./lb.	3	Remove packaging. Place roast on roasting rack. Microwave until wooden pick can be easily inserted in center, turning over after half the time.* Let stand for 10 to 15 min.
bone-in	9 to 12 min./lb.	3	Same as above.
Sirloin Chops	4 to 6 min./lb.	5	Remove packaging. Place chops on roasting rack. Microwave until pliable, breaking apart and rearranging as soon as possible.* Let stand for 5 to 10 min.
Rib Chops	4 to 6 min./lb.	5	Remove packaging. Place ribs on roasting rack. Microwave until pliable, breaking apart and rearranging as soon as possible.* Let stand for 5 to 10 min.
Stew Meat	5 to 7 min./lb.	5	Remove packaging. Place lamb on plate. Microwave until wooden pick can be easily inserted in each piece, breaking apart and rearranging as soon as possible. Let stand for 5 to 10 min.
Ground Lamb	5 to 7 min./lb.	5	Remove packaging. Place lamb on plate. Microwave, breaking apart and removing defrosted portions as soon as possible. Let stand for 5 to 10 min.

*Shield warm areas as necessary, page 12.

LAMB COOKING GUIDE

ITEM	TOTAL COOKING TIME	INTERNAL TEMP.*	POWER LEVEL	METHOD
Roast, boneless under 5 lbs.	Rare: 11 to 13 min./lb. Med: 12½ to 14½ min./lb. Well: 14 to 16 min./lb.	120°F 135°F 150°F	HIGH for first 5 min. of total time, then 5	Place roast, fat-side down, on roasting rack. Microwave to desired temp., turning over after half the time. Cover loosely with aluminum foil. Let stand for 10 min.
over 5 lbs.	Rare: 11 to 13 min./lb. Med: 12½ to 14½ min./lb. Well: 14 to 16 min./lb.	120°F 135°F 150°F	HIGH for first 8 min. of total time, then 5	Same as above.
Roast, bone-in under 5 lbs.	Rare: 11 to 13 min./lb. Med: 12½ to 14½ min./lb. Well: 14 to 16 min./lb.	120°F 135°F 150°F	HIGH for first 5 min. of total time, then 5	Place roast, fat-side down, on roasting rack. Microwave to desired temp., turning over after half the time. Cover loosely with aluminum foil. Let stand for 10 min.
over 5 lbs.	Rare: 11 to 13 min./lb. Med: 12½ to 14½ min./lb. Well: 14 to 16 min./lb.	120°F 135°F 150°F	HIGH for first 8 min. of total time, then 5	Same as above.

*Use temperature probe, if desired.

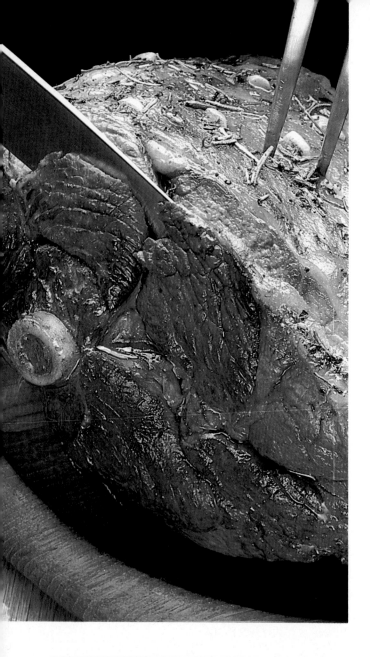

◁

GARLIC HERB LEG OF LAMB

Power Levels / HIGH, **5**
Approx. Cooking Time / 1 hour
Yield / 6 to 8 servings

3½ to 4-lb. bone-in sirloin half of leg of lamb
  3 cloves garlic, cut into slivers
  2 teaspoons dried rosemary leaves, crushed
  ½ teaspoon dried tarragon leaves
  ¼ teaspoon ground sage

1 Prepare leg of lamb according to photo directions below.

2 Place lamb, fat-side down, on roasting rack. Microwave at HIGH for 5 minutes.

3 Reduce to POWER LEVEL **5**. Microwave for 40 to 55 minutes longer, or until lamb is desired doneness, turning over and rubbing with remaining herb mixture after half the time. Cover loosely with aluminum foil. Let stand for 10 minutes.

GARLIC HERB LAMB ROAST

Follow recipe above, substituting a 3 to 3½-lb. boneless lamb roast for leg of lamb.

HOW TO PREPARE GARLIC HERB LEG OF LAMB

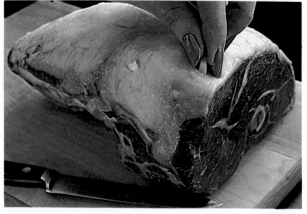

CUT several small slits in surface of lamb. Insert a garlic sliver into each slit.

MIX remaining ingredients in small bowl. Rub about half the herb mixture onto lamb. Continue as directed in step 2 above.

PERSIAN LAMB ▷

Power Levels / HIGH, **5**
Approx. Cooking Time / 1 hour 5 minutes
Yield / 4 to 6 servings

  1 can (16 oz.) peach slices
1½ lbs. boneless lamb stew meat, cut into 1-inch
     cubes
  ½ cup water
  1 tablespoon instant chicken bouillon granules
  1 tablespoon instant minced onion
  1 tablespoon lemon juice
  ¼ teaspoon ground cinnamon
  ⅛ teaspoon ground cloves
  ¼ cup raisins
  2 tablespoons water
  1 tablespoon cornstarch

1 Drain peach slices, reserving ½ cup juice.
Set peach slices aside. In 2-quart casserole,
mix reserved juice, lamb, ½ cup water,
the bouillon granules, onion, lemon juice,
cinnamon and cloves. Cover. Microwave at
HIGH for 5 minutes. Reduce to POWER
LEVEL **5**. Microwave for 45 to 55 minutes
longer, or until lamb is tender. Stir in raisins
and peach slices.

2 In small bowl, blend 2 tablespoons water
and the cornstarch. Stir into lamb mixture.
Microwave at HIGH for 4 to 5 minutes, or until
sauce thickens, stirring once. Let stand for 5 to
10 minutes.

GREEK LAMB CHOPS

Power Level / **8**
Approx. Cooking Time / 13 minutes
Yield / 4 servings

  1 teaspoon instant beef bouillon granules
  ½ teaspoon lemon pepper seasoning
  ½ teaspoon dried rosemary leaves, crushed
  ¼ teaspoon ground oregano
  ⅛ teaspoon garlic powder
  8 rib lamb chops, 1 inch thick (about 2 lbs.)

1 In small bowl, mix all ingredients except
chops. Slash fat at 2-inch intervals on edge of
each chop. Rub both sides of chops with
herb mixture.

2 Arrange chops on roasting rack. Microwave at
POWER LEVEL **8** for 11 to 13 minutes, or
until chops are desired doneness, rearranging
after half the time. Let stand for 2 to 3 minutes.

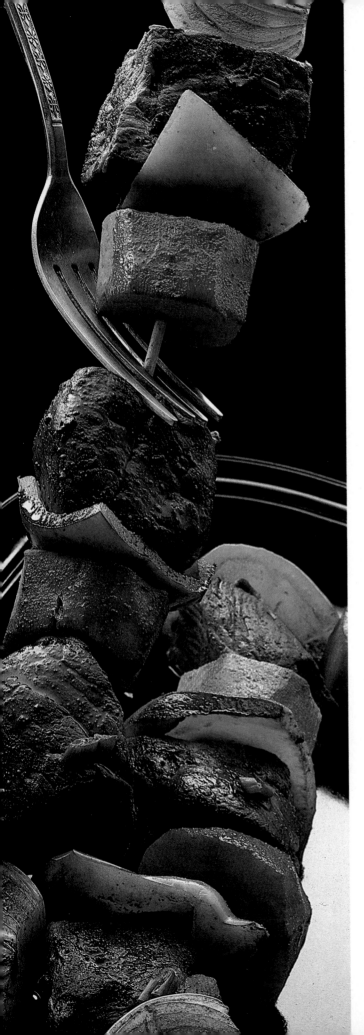

◁

LEMON MINT LAMB KABOBS

Power Levels / HIGH, **8**
Approx. Cooking Time / 26 minutes
Yield / 4 servings

1 cup water
¾ cup finely-chopped onion
½ cup lemon juice
2 tablespoons packed brown sugar
1 teaspoon ground coriander (optional)
1 teaspoon dried mint flakes
½ teaspoon ground turmeric (optional)
1 bay leaf
1 to 1½ lbs. boneless leg of lamb, cut into 1½-inch
    cubes
1 medium yam, peeled and cut into 1 x 1½-inch
    chunks
2 tablespoons water
4 small onions, cut in half
1 large green pepper, cored, seeded and cut into
    1½-inch pieces

1 In medium mixing bowl, mix 1 cup water,
   ¾ cup chopped onion, the lemon juice, brown
   sugar, coriander, mint, turmeric and bay leaf.
   Microwave at HIGH for 8 to 10 minutes, or
   until onion is tender and flavors are blended.
   Cool slightly.

2 Stir in lamb. Cover. Marinate in refrigerator for
   3 to 6 hours, stirring 1 or 2 times.

3 In small mixing bowl, combine yam and
   2 tablespoons water. Cover bowl with plastic
   wrap. Microwave at HIGH for 3 to 5 minutes,
   or until yam is tender.

4 Remove lamb from marinade with slotted
   spoon, reserving marinade. On each of four
   12-inch wooden skewers, thread 1 onion half.
   Then alternately thread lamb, green pepper
   and yam. Thread 1 onion half on end of each
   skewer. Arrange kabobs on roasting rack.
   Brush with marinade. Microwave at POWER
   LEVEL **8** for 9 to 11 minutes, or until lamb is
   desired doneness, rearranging and brushing
   kabobs with marinade after half the time.

FRENCH LAMB STEW ▽

Power Levels / HIGH, **5**
Approx. Cooking Time / 1 hour 15 minutes
Yield / 8 to 10 servings

 3 tablespoons all-purpose flour
 1 teaspoon salt
 ½ teaspoon dried oregano leaves
 ¼ teaspoon dried rosemary leaves
 2 lbs. boneless lamb stew meat, cut into 1-inch
    cubes
 1 can (28 oz.) whole tomatoes, undrained, cut up
 1 small eggplant, peeled and cut into ½-inch cubes
 1 medium green pepper, cored, seeded and
    chopped
 ½ cup white wine
 2 tablespoons lemon juice
 1½ teaspoons sugar
 2 cloves garlic, minced

1 In large plastic food storage bag, combine
   flour, salt, oregano and rosemary. Add lamb.
   Shake to coat. Transfer lamb and any
   remaining flour mixture to 3-quart casserole.

2 Stir in remaining ingredients. Cover. Microwave at HIGH for 5 minutes. Stir. Re-cover.

3 Reduce to POWER LEVEL **5**. Microwave for
   60 to 70 minutes longer, or until lamb is
   tender, stirring occasionally. Let stand for 5 to
   10 minutes.

CLASSIC LAMB CURRY ▽

Power Levels / HIGH, **5**
Approx. Cooking Time / 1 hour 4 minutes
Yield / 4 servings

 ¾ cup chopped onion
 2 tablespoons butter or margarine
 2 tablespoons all-purpose flour
 1 lb. boneless lamb stew meat, cut into 1-inch
    cubes
 1 cup chicken broth
 ⅓ cup flaked coconut
 ⅓ cup raisins or roasted peanuts
 1 to 1½ tablespoons curry powder
 1 tablespoon lemon juice
 ½ teaspoon ground ginger
 ½ teaspoon salt
    Hot cooked rice, page 122 (optional)

1 In 2-quart casserole, combine onion and
   butter. Microwave at HIGH for 3 to 4 minutes,
   or until onion is tender, stirring once.

2 Blend in flour. Stir in remaining ingredients
   except rice. Cover. Microwave at HIGH for
   5 minutes.

3 Reduce to POWER LEVEL **5**. Microwave for
   45 to 55 minutes longer, or until lamb is
   tender, stirring occasionally. Let stand for 5 to
   10 minutes. Serve with rice.

POULTRY DEFROSTING GUIDE

ITEM	TOTAL DEFROSTING TIME	POWER LEVEL	METHOD
Chicken whole	4 to 6 min./lb.	**5**	Remove packaging. Place chicken on roasting rack. Microwave until pliable, turning over and rotating after half the time.* Rinse cavity with cool water. Remove giblets. Let stand for 5 to 10 min.
pieces	5 to 8 min./lb.	**5**	Remove packaging. Place chicken on roasting rack. Microwave until pliable, breaking apart and rearranging as soon as possible. Let stand for 5 to 10 min.
breasts, boneless	6 to 8 min./lb.	**5**	Same as above.
Cornish Hen(s)	5 to 7 min./lb.	**5**	Remove packaging. Place hen(s) on roasting rack. Microwave until pliable, turning over and rearranging after half the time.* Rinse cavity with cool water. Remove giblets. Let stand for 5 to 10 min.
Duckling	4 to 6 min./lb.	**5**	Remove packaging. Place duckling on roasting rack. Microwave for half the time, rotating once. Rotate again, turn duck over and let stand for 10 minutes. Microwave until pliable, rotating once.* Submerge in cool water for 20 to 30 min., or until giblets can be removed. Let stand for 10 to 15 min.
Turkey whole 8 to 12 lbs.	4 to 7 min./lb.	**5**	Remove packaging. Place turkey on roasting rack. Microwave for ¼ of time. Turn turkey over. Microwave for second ¼ of time.* Turn turkey on its side. Microwave for third ¼ of time. Turn turkey to other side. Microwave until turkey is pliable yet slightly icy in cavity. Submerge in cool water for 20 to 30 minutes, or until giblets can be removed. Let stand for 10 min.
pieces	6 to 8 min./lb.	**5**	Remove packaging. Place turkey on roasting rack. Microwave until pliable, breaking apart and rearranging as soon as possible. Let stand for 5 to 10 min.
breast	5 to 7 min./lb.	**5**	Remove packaging. Place turkey breast on roasting rack. Microwave until pliable, turning over and rotating after half the time.* Let stand for 10 to 15 min.

*Shield warm areas as necessary, page 12.

POULTRY COOKING GUIDE

ITEM	TOTAL COOKING TIME	POWER LEVEL	METHOD
Chicken whole	9 to 12 min./lb.	**7**	Place chicken, breast-side down, on roasting rack. Microwave until meat near bone is no longer pink and juices run clear, turning over and rotating after half the time. Cover loosely with aluminum foil. Let stand for 5 to 10 min.
pieces	6 to 9 min./lb.	HIGH	Arrange chicken, bone-side down, on roasting rack. Microwave until meat near bone is no longer pink and juices run clear, rearranging after half the time. Cover loosely with aluminum foil. Let stand for 5 min.
Cornish Hen(s)	6 to 8 min./lb.	HIGH	Arrange hen(s), breast-side down, on roasting rack or baking sheet. Microwave until meat near bone is no longer pink and juices run clear, rotating rack 2 times, turning hens over after half the time and draining juices as necessary. Cover loosely with aluminum foil. Let stand for 5 min.
Duckling	7 to 9 min./lb.	HIGH for first 10 min. of total time, then **5**	Place duckling, breast-side down, on roasting rack. Microwave for 10 min. as directed. Turn duckling over. Microwave at **5** until meat near bone is no longer pink and juices run clear, rotating rack and draining juices 2 or 3 times. Cover loosely with aluminum foil. Let stand for 5 min.
Turkey whole 8 to 12 lbs.	13 to 16 min./lb.	HIGH for first 10 min. of total time, then **5**	Place turkey, breast-side down, in baking dish. Microwave for ¼ of total time.* Turn turkey on its side. Microwave for second ¼ of total time. Turn turkey to other side. Rotate rack. Microwave for third ¼ of total time. Turn turkey breast-side up. Microwave until meat near bone is no longer pink and juices run clear. Cover loosely with aluminum foil. Let stand for 15 to 30 min.
pieces	13 to 15 min./lb.	HIGH for first 5 min. of total time, then **5**	Arrange turkey, bone-side up, on roasting rack or baking sheet. Microwave until meat near bone is no longer pink and juices run clear, turning over and rearranging after half the time. Cover loosely with aluminum foil. Let stand for 5 min.
breast	13 to 16 min./lb.	HIGH for first 5 min. of total time, then **5**	Place turkey breast, skin-side down, in baking dish. Microwave until meat is no longer pink and juices run clear, rotating 2 times and turning over after half the time. Cover loosely with aluminum foil. Let stand for 10 to 15 min.

*Shield warm areas as necessary, page 12.

DUCKLING WITH ORANGE CURRANT GLAZE ◁

Power Levels / HIGH, **5**
Approx. Cooking Time / 45 minutes
Yield / 2 to 4 servings

½ **cup orange marmalade**
¼ **cup currant jelly**
⅛ **teaspoon pepper**
  Dash cinnamon
5 **to 5½-lb. duckling**

1 In small bowl, combine all ingredients except duckling. Microwave at HIGH for 1½ to 2 minutes, stirring every 30 seconds, or until marmalade and jelly melt. Set aside.

2 Place duckling, breast-side down, on roasting rack. Microwave at HIGH for 10 minutes.

3 Turn duckling over. Reduce to POWER LEVEL **5**. Microwave for 27 to 33 minutes longer, or until meat near bone is no longer pink, rotating rack and draining juices 2 or 3 times, and basting duckling with glaze during last 15 to 20 minutes. Cover loosely with aluminum foil. Let stand for 5 minutes.

ROSEMARY-SIMMERED CHICKEN

Power Level / **7**
Approx. Cooking Time / 25 minutes
Yield / 3 or 4 servings

1 **small onion, quartered**
2½ **to 3-lb. broiler-fryer chicken**
1 **cup chicken broth**
2 **cloves garlic, cut in half**
½ **teaspoon bouquet sauce**
½ **teaspoon dried rosemary leaves**
¼ **teaspoon dried thyme leaves**
⅛ **teaspoon pepper**
1 **bay leaf**

1 Place onion in cavity of chicken. With string, tie chicken legs together. Place in oven cooking bag. In small bowl, mix remaining ingredients. Pour over chicken. Tie bag loosely with string or nylon closure.

2 Place bag in 3-quart casserole. Microwave at POWER LEVEL **7** for 20 to 25 minutes, or until meat near bone is no longer pink and juices run clear, rotating casserole after half the time. Let stand for 5 minutes.

CORNISH HENS WITH APPLE SAUSAGE STUFFING ▷

Power Levels / HIGH, **5**
Approx. Cooking Time / 51 minutes
Yield / 4 servings

STUFFING

½ lb. bulk pork sausage
½ cup chopped celery
¼ cup chopped onion
3 cups unseasoned croutons
1 cup chopped apple
½ cup chicken broth
½ teaspoon poultry seasoning
½ teaspoon salt
⅛ teaspoon pepper

4 Cornish hens (about 1½ lbs. each)
3 tablespoons butter
1 teaspoon bouquet sauce

1 For stuffing, in 2-quart casserole, combine sausage, celery and onion. Microwave at HIGH for 2½ to 3½ minutes, or until sausage is no longer pink, stirring 1 or 2 times.

2 Stir in remaining stuffing ingredients. Cover. Microwave at POWER LEVEL **5** for 4½ to 5½ minutes, or until croutons are soft. Stuff each hen with an equal amount of stuffing. With string, tie legs of each hen together. Arrange hens, breast-side down, on baking sheet.

3 Place butter in small bowl. Microwave at HIGH for 45 to 60 seconds, or until butter melts. Stir in bouquet sauce.

4 Brush hens with half the butter mixture. Microwave at HIGH for 15 minutes, rotating baking sheet after half the time. Drain juices. Turn hens over. Brush with remaining butter mixture.

5 Microwave at HIGH for 24 to 26 minutes longer, or until meat near bone is no longer pink, rearranging hens 3 times. Let stand for 5 minutes.

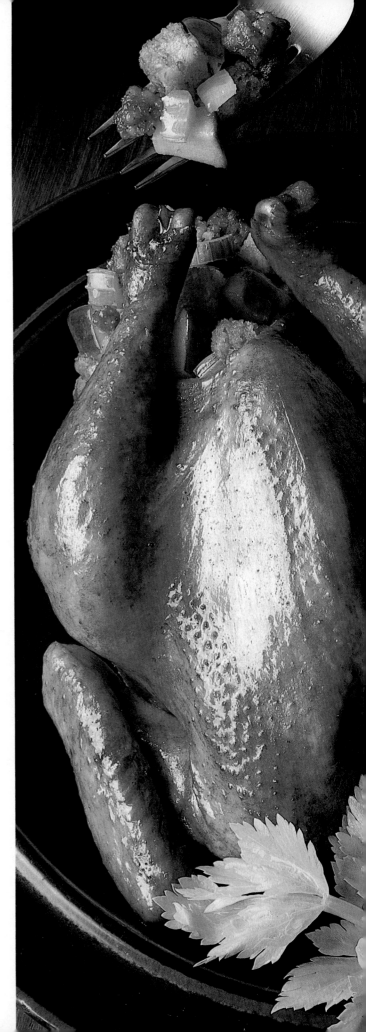

WESTERN CHICKEN ▽

Power Levels / HIGH, **7**
Approx. Cooking Time / 13 minutes
Yield / 4 servings

 2 **whole bone-in chicken breasts, split in half,
    skin removed**
 2 **teaspoons lemon juice**
 ¼ **teaspoon instant minced onion**
 ½ **teaspoon dried basil leaves**
 ⅛ **teaspoon pepper**
 ⅔ **cup shredded Cheddar cheese (about 2⅔ oz.)**
 ½ **small avocado, peeled and thinly sliced
    (optional)**
 4 **thin slices tomato**

1 Arrange chicken breasts, bone-side down,
   in 9-inch square baking dish. Sprinkle with
   lemon juice, onion, basil and pepper. Cover
   dish with wax paper. Microwave at HIGH for
   7½ to 9 minutes, or until meat near bone is no
   longer pink and juices run clear, rearranging
   after half the time.

2 Sprinkle chicken with half the Cheddar
   cheese. Top with avocado and tomato slices.
   Sprinkle with remaining cheese. Microwave at
   POWER LEVEL **7** for 3 to 4 minutes, or until
   cheese melts, rotating dish after half the time.
   Cover loosely with aluminum foil. Let stand
   for 5 minutes.

CHICKEN WITH CREAMY MUSHROOM SAUCE

Power Levels / HIGH, **5**
Approx. Cooking Time / 24 minutes
Yield / 4 to 6 servings

 3 **whole bone-in chicken breasts, split in half,
    skin removed**
 1 **medium onion, thinly sliced**
 1 **can (10¾ oz.) condensed cream of mushroom
    soup**
 1 **cup sliced fresh mushrooms**
 1 **cup dairy sour cream**
 1 **tablespoon sherry (optional)**
 1 **teaspoon dried parsley flakes**
 ½ **teaspoon salt**
 ⅛ **teaspoon pepper**
 ⅛ **teaspoon garlic powder**

1 Arrange chicken breasts, bone-side down, in
   12 x 8-inch baking dish. Arrange onion slices
   on top of chicken. Cover dish with plastic
   wrap. Microwave at HIGH for 12 to 14
   minutes, or until meat near bone is no longer
   pink, rearranging after half the time.

2 Drain cooking juices into medium mixing
   bowl. Stir in remaining ingredients. Pour over
   chicken. Microwave at POWER LEVEL **5** for 8
   to 10 minutes, or until sauce is heated through
   and mushrooms are tender, rotating dish after
   half the time.

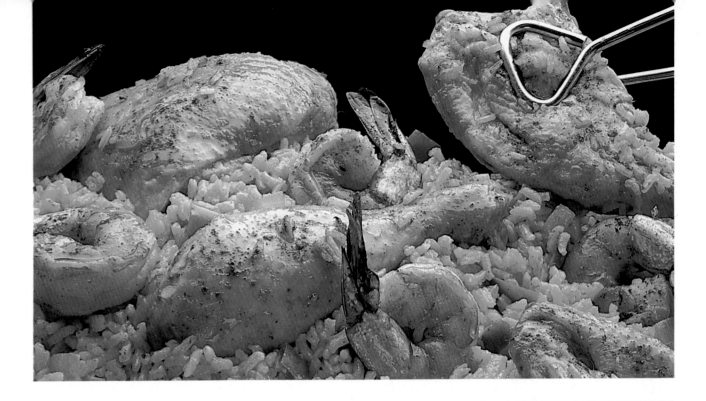

EASY PAELLA △

Power Levels / HIGH, 🎱
Approx. Cooking Time / 35 minutes
Yield / 6 to 8 servings

  1 medium onion, chopped
  ½ cup chopped green pepper
  2 tablespoons olive oil
  1 clove garlic, minced
2⅓ cups uncooked instant rice
  1 can (14½ oz.) chicken broth
  ½ teaspoon ground turmeric
  ½ teaspoon salt
  ¼ teaspoon pepper
2½ to 3-lb. broiler-fryer chicken, cut up
    Paprika
  ½ lb. fresh medium shrimp, peeled and deveined,
    page 27

1 In 3-quart casserole, combine onion, green
pepper, oil and garlic. Microwave at HIGH for
4 to 5 minutes, or until onion is tender. Stir in
rice, broth, turmeric, salt and pepper.

2 Arrange chicken pieces, bone-side up, on top
of rice mixture. Sprinkle lightly with paprika.
Cover. Microwave at POWER LEVEL 🎱 for
15 minutes. Remove chicken pieces; set aside.

3 Stir shrimp into rice mixture. Replace chicken,
bone-side down, on rice mixture. Sprinkle
lightly with paprika. Re-cover. Microwave at
POWER LEVEL 🎱 for 12 to 15 minutes, or
until chicken meat near bone is no longer
pink. Let stand for 10 minutes.

BRUNSWICK STEW

Power Levels / HIGH, 🎱
Approx. Cooking Time / 40 minutes
Yield / 4 to 6 servings

2½ to 3-lb. broiler-fryer chicken, cut up
  2 cups water
  2 teaspoons instant minced onion
  1 teaspoon salt
  2 bay leaves
  ¼ teaspoon whole black peppercorns
  1 can (16 oz.) whole tomatoes, undrained, cut up
  1 pkg. (10 oz.) frozen mixed vegetables
  1 pkg. (10 oz.) frozen sliced okra

1 In 3-quart casserole, combine chicken, water,
onion, salt, bay leaves and peppercorns.
Cover. Microwave at HIGH for 7 minutes.

2 Reduce to POWER LEVEL 🎱. Microwave for
12 to 15 minutes longer, or until meat near
bone is no longer pink, rearranging after half
the time.

3 Remove and discard bay leaves and peppercorns. Remove chicken; set aside. Add
remaining ingredients to cooking liquid.
Re-cover. Microwave at HIGH for 12 to 15
minutes, or until vegetables are tender,
stirring once.

4 Meanwhile, remove chicken meat from skin
and bones. Discard skin and bones. Cut meat
into bite-size pieces. Stir into vegetables.
Microwave at POWER LEVEL 🎱 for 3
minutes, or until hot.

CHEESY CHICKEN WITH CHIVES ▽

Power Levels / HIGH, **9**
Approx. Cooking Time / 17 minutes
Yield / 4 servings

⅓ cup butter or margarine
½ cup cornflake crumbs
¼ cup grated Parmesan cheese
1½ teaspoons freeze-dried chives
1½ teaspoons dried parsley flakes
2½ to 3-lb. broiler-fryer chicken, cut up
    (remove skin if desired)

1 Place butter in shallow dish. Microwave at HIGH for 45 seconds to 1¼ minutes, or until butter melts.

2 In another shallow dish or on sheet of wax paper, mix cornflake crumbs, Parmesan cheese, chives and parsley flakes. Dip chicken pieces in butter, then in crumb mixture to coat.

3 Arrange chicken pieces, bone-side down, on roasting rack. Microwave at POWER LEVEL **9** for 13 to 16 minutes, or until meat near bone is no longer pink and juices run clear, rearranging after half the time. Let stand for 5 minutes.

HERBED LEMON CHICKEN

Power Level / HIGH
Approx. Cooking Time / 15 minutes
Yield / 4 servings

2½ to 3-lb. broiler-fryer chicken, cut up
 1 teaspoon garlic salt
 1 teaspoon paprika
 1 teaspoon grated lemon peel
 ½ teaspoon dried oregano leaves
 ¼ teaspoon pepper
 2 tablespoons lemon juice
 1 can (4 oz.) sliced mushrooms, drained (optional)

1 Arrange chicken pieces, bone-side down, in 12 x 8-inch baking dish. In small bowl, mix garlic salt, paprika, lemon peel, oregano and pepper. Rub onto chicken pieces. Sprinkle chicken with lemon juice. Top with mushrooms.

2 Cover dish with wax paper. Microwave at HIGH for 12 to 15 minutes, or until meat near bone is no longer pink and juices run clear, rearranging after half the time. Let stand for 5 minutes.

HERB-BASTED TURKEY BREAST

Power Levels / HIGH, **5**
Approx. Cooking Time / 1 hour 51 minutes
Yield / 6 to 8 servings

 2 tablespoons butter or margarine
 ½ teaspoon poultry seasoning
 ¼ teaspoon dried thyme leaves
 ¼ teaspoon pepper
 ⅛ teaspoon garlic powder
 6 to 6½-lb. turkey breast

1 Place butter in small bowl. Microwave at HIGH for 45 to 60 seconds, or until butter melts. Stir in remaining ingredients except turkey breast.

2 Place turkey breast, skin-side down, in 12 x 8-inch baking dish. Brush with half the butter mixture. Microwave at HIGH for 5 minutes.

3 Reduce to POWER LEVEL **5**. Microwave for 1¼ to 1¾ hours longer, or until meat near bone is no longer pink and juices run clear, turning turkey over, brushing with remaining butter mixture and rotating dish after half the time. Cover loosely with aluminum foil. Let stand for 10 to 15 minutes.

CHICKEN PARMESAN

Power Levels / **9**, HIGH, **7**
Approx. Cooking Time / 20 minutes
Yield / 4 to 6 servings

¼ **cup water**
1 **egg**
¾ **cup seasoned dry bread crumbs**
¼ **cup grated Parmesan cheese**
¼ **teaspoon paprika**
3 **whole boneless chicken breasts, split in half,**
   skin removed
1 **can (8 oz.) tomato sauce**
1 **can (7½ oz.) whole tomatoes, drained**
1 **teaspoon sugar**
½ **teaspoon dried oregano leaves**
⅛ **teaspoon garlic powder**
1 **can (4 oz.) sliced mushrooms, drained**
1 **cup shredded mozzarella cheese (about 4 oz.)**

1 In shallow dish, blend water and egg. Set
   aside. In another shallow dish or on sheet of
   wax paper, mix bread crumbs, Parmesan
   cheese and paprika. Dip each chicken piece in
   egg, then in bread crumb mixture to coat.

2 Arrange chicken pieces on roasting rack.
   Microwave at POWER LEVEL **9** for 11 to 13
   minutes, or until chicken is no longer pink,
   rearranging pieces and rotating rack 2 times.
   Set aside.

3 In 1-quart casserole, combine tomato sauce,
   tomatoes, sugar, oregano and garlic powder.
   Stir to blend and break apart tomatoes. Cover
   dish with wax paper. Microwave at HIGH for
   2 minutes. Stir in mushrooms.

4 Arrange chicken pieces in 9-inch square
   baking dish. Pour tomato mixture over
   chicken. Sprinkle with mozzarella cheese.
   Microwave at POWER LEVEL **7** for 4 to 5
   minutes, or until cheese melts, rotating
   dish once.

QUICK CHICKEN AND VEGETABLES △

Power Level / HIGH
Approx. Cooking Time / 12 minutes
Yield / 3 or 4 servings

1 **medium onion, sliced**
½ **cup thinly-sliced celery**
½ **cup thinly-sliced carrot**
3 **tablespoons butter or margarine**
2 **tablespoons all-purpose flour**
1½ **teaspoons instant chicken bouillon granules**
¼ **teaspoon dried marjoram leaves**
⅛ **teaspoon dried thyme leaves**
⅛ **teaspoon pepper**
1 **cup hot water**
1 **whole boneless chicken breast, skin removed,**
   cut into thin strips
   Hot cooked noodles, page 122 (optional)

1 In 1½-quart casserole, combine onion, celery,
   carrot and butter. Cover. Microwave at HIGH
   for 5 to 6 minutes, or until vegetables are
   tender, stirring once.

2 Stir in flour, bouillon granules, marjoram,
   thyme and pepper. Blend in water. Stir in
   chicken. Cover. Microwave at HIGH for 5 to 6
   minutes, or until chicken is no longer pink,
   stirring once. Let stand for 3 to 5 minutes.
   Serve with noodles.

◁

TURKEY TETRAZZINI

Power Levels / HIGH, **7**
Approx. Cooking Time / 19 minutes
Yield / 4 to 6 servings

 2 tablespoons butter or margarine
⅓ cup seasoned dry bread crumbs
¼ cup butter or margarine
¼ cup all-purpose flour
½ teaspoon Italian seasoning
½ teaspoon salt
¼ teaspoon pepper
 1 cup chicken broth
 1 cup half-and-half
 1 tablespoon sherry (optional)
 1 pkg. (8 oz.) spaghetti, cooked, page 122
 2 cups cut-up cooked turkey
 1 can (4 oz.) sliced mushrooms, drained
¼ cup grated Parmesan cheese

1 Place 2 tablespoons butter in small bowl. Microwave at HIGH for 45 to 60 seconds, or until butter melts. Stir in bread crumbs. Set aside.

2 Place ¼ cup butter in 2-quart casserole. Microwave at HIGH for 45 seconds to 1¼ minutes, or until butter melts.

3 Blend flour, Italian seasoning, salt and pepper into butter. Stir in broth and half-and-half. Microwave at POWER LEVEL **7** for 8 to 9 minutes, or until mixture thickens, stirring every 2 minutes. Blend in sherry.

4 Stir in spaghetti, turkey, mushrooms and Parmesan cheese. Cover. Microwave at POWER LEVEL **7** for 5 to 6 minutes, or until heated through, stirring once.

5 Sprinkle with bread crumb mixture. Microwave, uncovered, at POWER LEVEL **7** for about 2 minutes, or until hot.

CHICKEN TETRAZZINI

Follow recipe above, substituting cooked chicken for turkey.

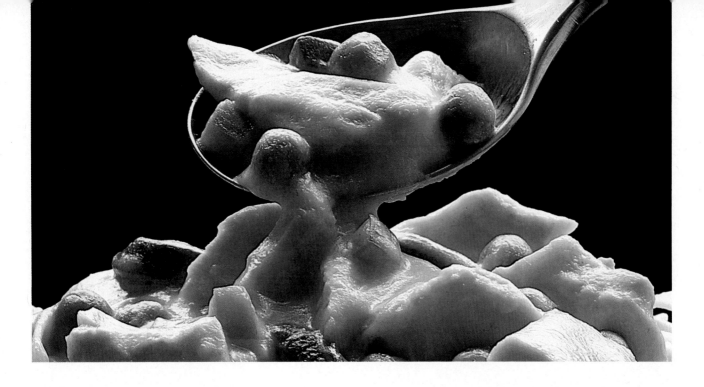

CHICKEN À LA KING △

Power Levels / HIGH, **7**
Approx. Cooking Time / 18 minutes
Yield / 4 servings

¼ cup butter or margarine
 2 tablespoons finely-chopped green pepper
¼ cup all-purpose flour
½ teaspoon salt
⅛ teaspoon pepper
 1 cup chicken broth
 1 cup milk
 2 cups cut-up cooked chicken
½ cup frozen green peas
 1 jar (2 oz.) sliced pimiento, drained
 2 tablespoons sherry (optional)
   Toast, hot cooked noodles or rice, page 122

1 In 2-quart casserole, combine butter and green pepper. Microwave at HIGH for 3 to 4 minutes, or until green pepper is tender.

2 Blend in flour, salt and pepper. Gradually stir in broth and milk. Microwave at POWER LEVEL **7** for 6 to 7 minutes, or until sauce thickens, stirring 2 or 3 times.

3 Stir in chicken, peas, pimiento and sherry. Microwave at POWER LEVEL **7** for 6 to 7 minutes, or until heated through, stirring 2 times. Serve over toast.

TURKEY À LA KING

Follow recipe above, substituting cooked turkey for chicken.

CHICKEN AMANDINE

Power Levels / HIGH, **5**
Approx. Cooking Time / 14 minutes
Yield / 4 servings

½ cup sliced almonds
 3 tablespoons butter or margarine
 3 tablespoons all-purpose flour
 1 tablespoon dried parsley flakes
½ teaspoon salt
⅛ teaspoon pepper
⅛ teaspoon garlic powder
 1 cup half-and-half
½ cup chicken broth
¼ cup white wine
 2 cups cut-up cooked chicken
   Hot cooked egg noodles, page 122

1 In 2-quart casserole, combine almonds and butter. Microwave at HIGH for 4 to 5 minutes, or until almonds lightly brown, stirring after every minute. Remove almonds with slotted spoon, reserving butter. Drain almonds on paper towels; set aside.

2 Blend flour, parsley flakes, salt, pepper and garlic powder into reserved butter. Stir in half-and-half, broth and wine. Microwave at POWER LEVEL **5** for 5 to 7 minutes, or until mixture thickens, stirring after every minute.

3 Stir in chicken. Microwave at POWER LEVEL **5** for 1 to 2 minutes, or until heated through. Stir in almonds. Serve with noodles.

FISH & SEAFOOD

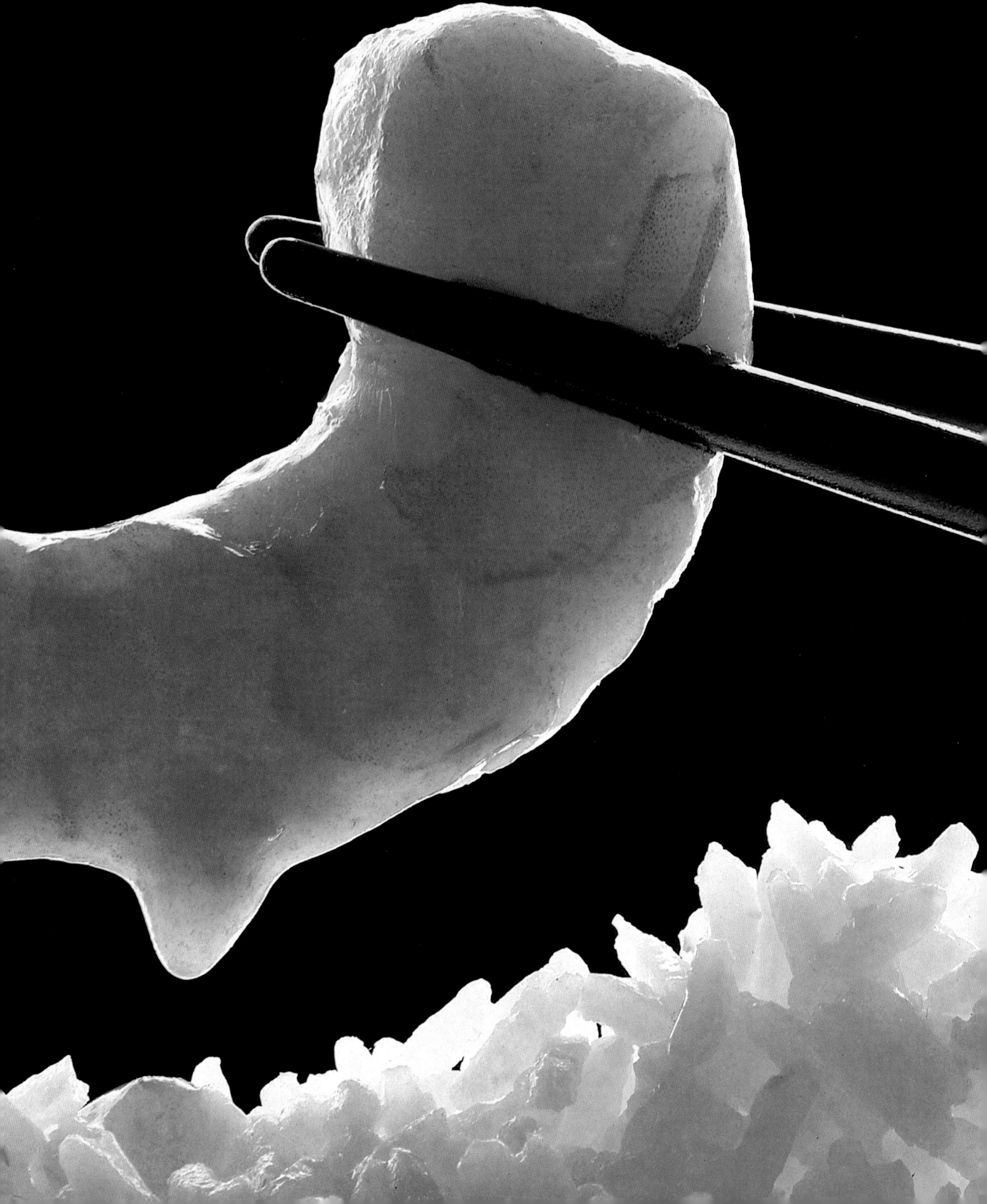

FISH AND SEAFOOD DEFROSTING GUIDE

ITEM	TOTAL DEFROSTING TIME	POWER LEVEL	METHOD
Fish whole	9 to 11 min./lb.	**5**	Remove packaging. Place fish on roasting rack. Shield head and tail with aluminum foil, page 12. Microwave until pliable, turning over after half the time. Let stand for 10 to 15 min.
steaks	4½ to 6 min./lb.	**5**	Remove packaging. Place steaks on roasting rack. Microwave until wooden pick can be easily inserted in center of each steak, breaking apart, turning over and rearranging as soon as possible.* Let stand for 5 to 10 min.
fillets	5 to 7½ min./lb.	**5**	Remove packaging. Place fillets on roasting rack. Microwave until pliable, breaking apart and rearranging as soon as possible.* Let stand for 5 to 10 min.
Scallops	3½ to 6 min./lb.	**5**	Remove packaging. Place seafood on plate. Microwave until pliable, breaking apart and rearranging as soon as possible. Let stand for 5 to 10 min.
Shrimp	3 to 5 min./lb.	**5**	Same as above.

*Shield warm areas as necessary, page 12.

FISH AND SEAFOOD COOKING GUIDE

ITEM	TOTAL COOKING TIME	POWER LEVEL	METHOD
Fish whole	8 to 10 min./lb.	**5**	Place fish on roasting rack. Microwave until fish flakes easily with fork, turning over after half the time. Let stand for 3 to 5 min.
steaks	10 to 13 min./lb.	**5**	Arrange steaks on roasting rack with meaty portions toward outside of rack. Cover rack with wax paper. Microwave until fish flakes easily with fork, turning over and rearranging after half the time. Let stand for 3 to 5 min.
fillets	5½ to 8½ min./lb.	HIGH	Arrange fillets in baking dish. Cover dish with wax paper. Microwave until fish flakes easily with fork, turning over and rearranging after half the time. Let stand for 2 to 3 min.
Scallops	4 to 7 min./lb.	HIGH	Arrange seafood in baking dish. Cover dish with wax paper. Microwave until firm and opaque, stirring after half the time. Let stand for 5 min.
Shrimp	4 to 6 min./lb.	HIGH	Same as above.

POACHED FISH FILLETS ▷

Power Level / HIGH
Approx. Cooking Time / 8 minutes
Yield / 4 to 6 servings

**1½ lbs. fish fillets, about ½ inch thick
2 tablespoons finely-chopped onion
½ cup white wine or chicken broth**

1 Arrange fillets in 12 x 8-inch baking dish
   with thicker portions toward outside of dish.
   Sprinkle with onion. Pour wine over fillets.
   Cover dish with plastic wrap.

2 Microwave at HIGH for 6 to 8 minutes, or until
   fish flakes easily with fork, rotating dish every
   2 minutes. Let stand for 5 minutes.

MANDARIN SHRIMP AND PEAPODS

Power Levels / HIGH, **7**
Approx. Cooking Time / 19 minutes
Yield / 4 servings

**1 pkg. (6 oz.) frozen peapods
1 can (11 oz.) mandarin orange segments
½ cup chicken broth
½ cup chopped green onion
3 tablespoons chili sauce
1 tablespoon plus 1½ teaspoons cornstarch
⅛ teaspoon white pepper
⅛ teaspoon garlic powder
1 lb. fresh medium shrimp, peeled and deveined,
     page 27
1 can (8 oz.) sliced water chestnuts, drained
Hot cooked rice, page 122**

1 Remove peapods from packaging and place on
   plate. Microwave at HIGH for 3 to 4 minutes.
   Let stand for 5 minutes. Set aside.

2 Drain mandarin orange juice into 2-quart
   casserole. Set orange segments aside. Blend
   broth, onion, chili sauce, cornstarch, white
   pepper and garlic powder into juice. Microwave at HIGH for 3½ to 5½ minutes, or until
   sauce thickens and becomes translucent,
   stirring after every minute.

3 Stir in peapods, shrimp and water chestnuts.
   Microwave at POWER LEVEL **7** for 8 to 10
   minutes, or until shrimp are firm and opaque,
   stirring every 2 minutes. Stir in orange
   segments. Let stand for 3 minutes. Serve
   with rice.

ROLLED FISH FILLETS WITH VEGETABLES △

Power Level / HIGH
Approx. Cooking Time / 10 minutes
Yield / 4 to 6 servings

  2 small onions, thinly sliced
  2 tablespoons butter or margarine
  1 clove garlic, minced
1½ cups sliced fresh mushrooms
  1 can (16 oz.) whole tomatoes, drained, cut up
¼ cup white wine
¼ teaspoon dried basil leaves
1½ lbs. fish fillets (4 to 6 fillets), about ½ inch thick

1 In 12 x 8-inch baking dish, combine onions, butter and garlic. Cover dish with plastic wrap. Microwave at HIGH for 3½ to 4½ minutes, or until onions are tender. Stir in mushrooms, tomatoes, wine and basil.

2 Roll up each fillet, starting with narrow end. Secure ends with wooden picks. Arrange on vegetable mixture. Re-cover. Microwave at HIGH for 5 to 6 minutes, or until fish flakes easily with fork, turning fillets over and rotating dish after half the time. Let stand for 5 minutes. Spoon vegetables over fillets when serving.

FISHERMAN'S SPECIAL

Power Level / HIGH
Approx. Cooking Time / 19 minutes
Yield / 4 to 6 servings

½ cup thinly-sliced celery
½ cup chopped onion
  1 clove garlic, minced
  1 can (28 oz.) whole tomatoes, undrained, cut up
  1 cup water
¼ cup white wine
  1 teaspoon dried parsley flakes
  1 teaspoon instant chicken bouillon granules
  1 teaspoon salt
  1 teaspoon sugar
⅛ teaspoon dried thyme leaves
  1 lb. fish fillets, about ½ inch thick, cut into 1-inch chunks

1 In 2-quart casserole, combine celery, onion and garlic. Cover. Microwave at HIGH for 4 to 5 minutes, or until vegetables are tender, stirring once.

2 Stir in remaining ingredients except fish. Re-cover. Microwave at HIGH for 10 minutes, stirring once.

3 Stir in fish. Re-cover. Microwave at HIGH for 3 to 4 minutes, or until fish flakes easily with fork. Let stand for 5 minutes.

COQUILLE NEWFOUNDLAND

Power Levels / HIGH, **7**
Approx. Cooking Time / 14 minutes
Yield / 4 servings

 2 tablespoons butter or margarine
¼ cup unseasoned dry bread crumbs
½ teaspoon dried parsley flakes
 1 lb. scallops*
¼ cup white wine
 2 tablespoons butter or margarine
 2 tablespoons chopped green onion
 2 tablespoons all-purpose flour
   Dash white pepper
 1 cup sliced fresh mushrooms
¾ cup half-and-half
⅓ cup shredded Swiss cheese (about 1⅓ oz.)

1 Place 2 tablespoons butter in small bowl.
   Microwave at HIGH for 45 to 60 seconds, or
   until butter melts. Stir in bread crumbs and
   parsley flakes. Set aside.

2 In 1-quart casserole, combine scallops and
   wine. Cover. Microwave at POWER LEVEL **7**
   for 4 to 5 minutes, or until scallops are firm
   and opaque, stirring 2 or 3 times. Drain
   cooking liquid, reserving ¼ cup. Re-cover
   scallops; set aside.

3 In 1½-quart casserole, combine 2 tablespoons
   butter and the onion. Microwave at HIGH for
   1½ to 2 minutes, or until onion is tender.

4 Stir flour and white pepper into onion
   mixture. Blend in reserved cooking liquid,
   mushrooms and half-and-half. Microwave at
   POWER LEVEL **7** for 3 to 4 minutes, or until
   mixture thickens, stirring 3 times. Stir in
   scallops and Swiss cheese.

5 Sprinkle with bread crumb mixture. Microwave at POWER LEVEL **7** for 1 to 2 minutes,
   or until hot. Let stand for 2 to 3 minutes.

*Cut larger scallops into bite-size pieces.

EASY CRAB À LA KING ▽

Power Levels / HIGH, **7**
Approx. Cooking Time / 9 minutes
Yield / 4 to 6 servings

½ cup chopped celery
⅓ cup chopped onion
¼ cup chopped green pepper
 2 tablespoons butter or margarine
 2 pkgs. (6 oz. each) frozen crab meat, thawed
 3 hard-cooked eggs, chopped
¾ cup mayonnaise or salad dressing
 1 teaspoon Worcestershire sauce
½ teaspoon salt
⅛ teaspoon pepper
   Toast points

1 In 2-quart casserole, combine celery, onion,
   green pepper and butter. Microwave at
   HIGH for 2½ to 3½ minutes, or until
   vegetables are tender.

2 Stir in remaining ingredients except toast
   points. Cover. Microwave at POWER LEVEL
   7 for 5 to 6 minutes, or until heated through,
   stirring once. Serve over toast points.

SALMON STEAKS WITH DILL BUTTER △

Power Levels / HIGH, **5**
Approx. Cooking Time / 30 minutes
Yield / 4 servings

½ cup chopped celery
2 tablespoons butter or margarine
½ teaspoon dried dill weed
2 tablespoons butter or margarine
1 tablespoon snipped fresh parsley
½ teaspoon salt
¼ teaspoon pepper
¼ cup white wine
4 salmon steaks (about 2 lbs.)

1 In small mixing bowl, combine celery, 2 tablespoons butter and the dill weed. Microwave at HIGH for 3 to 4 minutes, or until celery is tender-crisp.

2 Add 2 tablespoons butter, the parsley, salt and pepper. Microwave at HIGH for 1 minute, or until butter melts. Stir in wine.

3 Arrange salmon steaks in 12 x 8-inch baking dish with meaty portions toward outside of dish. Spoon one-fourth of dill butter over steaks. Cover dish with wax paper. Microwave at POWER LEVEL **5** for about 10 minutes.

4 Rearrange and turn steaks over. Spoon one-third of remaining dill butter over steaks. Re-cover. Microwave at POWER LEVEL **5** for about 15 minutes longer, or until fish flakes easily with fork. Let stand for 5 minutes. Serve with remaining dill butter.

CREAMY SALMON TARRAGON BAKE

Power Levels / HIGH, **8**
Approx. Cooking Time / 16 minutes
Yield / 4 to 6 servings

1 tablespoon butter or margarine
¼ cup cornflake crumbs
1 can (16 oz.) salmon
1 carton (15 oz.) ricotta cheese
⅓ cup chopped green onion
2 teaspoons lemon juice
¾ to 1 teaspoon dried tarragon leaves
½ teaspoon salt
⅛ teaspoon pepper
¾ cup small shell macaroni, cooked, page 122

1 Place butter in small bowl. Microwave at HIGH for 45 to 60 seconds, or until butter melts. Stir in cornflake crumbs. Set aside.

2 Drain salmon, reserving ¼ cup liquid. Remove and discard skin and bones from salmon. In 1½-quart casserole, combine reserved liquid, ricotta cheese, onion, lemon juice, tarragon, salt and pepper. Stir in macaroni. Gently stir in salmon. Microwave at POWER LEVEL **8** for 5 minutes. Stir.

3 Sprinkle with cornflake crumb mixture. Microwave at POWER LEVEL **8** for 7 to 10 minutes, or until heated through and internal temperature registers 140°F.* Let stand for 3 minutes.

*Use temperature probe, if desired.

SHRIMP CREOLE △

Power Levels / HIGH, **7**
Approx. Cooking Time / 21 minutes
Yield / 4 servings

½ cup chopped celery
½ cup chopped green pepper
½ cup chopped onion
2 tablespoons vegetable oil
2 cloves garlic, minced
1 can (16 oz.) whole tomatoes, drained
1 can (16 oz.) tomato sauce
2 teaspoons sugar
1 teaspoon chili powder
½ teaspoon salt
¼ teaspoon pepper
⅛ teaspoon cayenne
1 lb. fresh medium shrimp, peeled and deveined,
   page 27
   Hot cooked rice, page 122

1 In 2-quart casserole, combine celery, green
   pepper, onion, oil and garlic. Microwave at
   HIGH for 3 to 5 minutes, or until vegetables
   are tender, stirring 2 times.

2 Add remaining ingredients except shrimp and
   rice. Stir to blend and break apart tomatoes.
   Microwave at HIGH for 5 to 7 minutes, or until
   flavors are blended, stirring once.

3 Stir in shrimp. Microwave at POWER LEVEL
   7 for 7 to 9 minutes, or until shrimp are firm
   and opaque, stirring every 2 minutes. Let
   stand for 5 minutes. Serve with rice.

CRUNCHY TUNA CASSEROLE

Power Levels / HIGH, **9**
Approx. Cooking Time / 11 minutes
Yield / 4 to 6 servings

1 tablespoon butter or margarine
1 tablespoon soy sauce
⅛ teaspoon garlic powder
1 can (3 oz.) chow mein noodles (about 2 cups)
1 can (10¾ oz.) condensed cream of mushroom
   soup
¾ cup milk
½ cup uncooked instant rice
1 can (7 oz.) tuna, drained and flaked
¼ cup slivered almonds
1½ teaspoons instant minced onion
⅛ teaspoon pepper

1 Place butter in small mixing bowl. Microwave
   at HIGH for 45 to 60 seconds, or until butter
   melts. Stir in soy sauce and garlic powder.
   Add noodles; toss to coat. Set aside.

2 In 2-quart casserole, combine remaining
   ingredients. Mix well. Cover. Microwave at
   HIGH for 8 to 9 minutes, or until rice is tender,
   stirring 2 times.

3 Sprinkle with chow mein noodles. Microwave, uncovered, at POWER LEVEL **9** for 1
   minute, or until hot. Let stand for 3 minutes.

EGGS & CHEESE

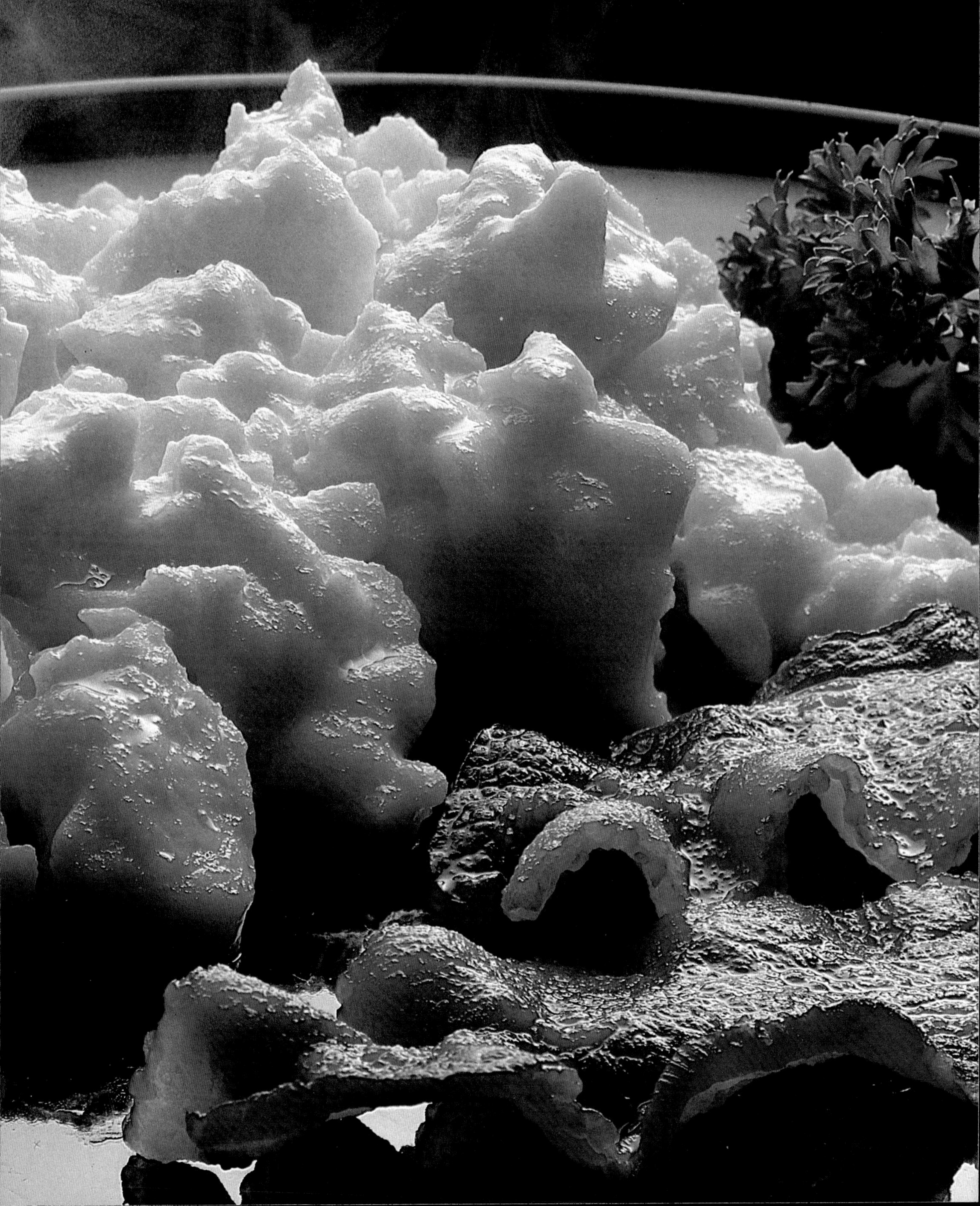

SCRAMBLED EGG GUIDE

EGG(S)	BUTTER	MILK/WATER	EGG COOKING TIME
1	1 teaspoon	1 tablespoon	45 to 60 seconds
2	2 teaspoons	1 tablespoon	1¼ to 1¾ minutes
4	1 tablespoon	2 tablespoons	3 to 3¾ minutes
8	2 tablespoons	¼ cup	4 to 4¾ minutes

HOW TO MAKE SCRAMBLED EGGS

PLACE butter in small bowl or casserole. Microwave at HIGH for 30 to 60 seconds, or until butter melts. Add egg(s) and milk. Beat until well blended.

MICROWAVE at HIGH as directed or until egg(s) are set yet moist, stirring 3 or 4 times. Let stand for 2 to 3 minutes. (Eggs will finish cooking during standing.)

POACHED EGG GUIDE

EGG(S)	WATER	VINEGAR	EGG COOKING TIME
1	2 tablespoons	¼ teaspoon	45 to 60 seconds
2	4 tablespoons, divided	½ teaspoon, divided	1 to 1½ minutes
4	8 tablespoons, divided	1 teaspoon, divided	2 to 2½ minutes

HOW TO MAKE POACHED EGGS

USING a 6-oz. custard cup for each egg, combine 2 tablespoons water and ¼ teaspoon vinegar in each cup. Microwave cup(s) at HIGH for 45 seconds to 2 minutes, or until mixture boils.

BREAK 1 egg into each cup. Cover cup(s) with plastic wrap. Microwave at POWER LEVEL **7** as directed, or until whites are opaque and yolks are slightly set. Let stand for 2 to 3 minutes. (Eggs will finish cooking during standing.)

FILLED FRENCH OMELET

Power Levels / HIGH, **7**, (**9**)
Approx. Cooking Time / 5 to 7 minutes
Yield / 2 to 4 servings

   **Apple Filling, Vegetable Filling or Cheesy Ham
     and Potato Filling, below**
1 **tablespoon butter or margarine**
4 **eggs, separated**
¼ **teaspoon salt**
⅛ **teaspoon pepper**

1 Prepare desired filling. Set aside.

2 Place butter in 9-inch pie plate. Microwave at
HIGH for 45 to 60 seconds, or until butter
melts. Tilt pie plate to coat sides and bottom.
Set aside.

3 Place egg whites in large mixing bowl. Beat at
high speed of electric mixer until soft peaks
form. In small bowl, combine egg yolks, salt
and pepper. Beat until well blended. Fold into
egg whites.

4 Spread egg mixture in prepared pie plate.
Microwave at POWER LEVEL **7** for 2½ to 3½
minutes, or until knife inserted in center
comes out clean. Spoon filling onto omelet.
Fold in half if desired.

APPLE FILLING

In small mixing bowl, combine 1 small baking
apple, peeled, cored and thinly sliced, 1 tablespoon butter or margarine, 1 tablespoon honey
and dash ground cinnamon. Cover bowl with
plastic wrap. Microwave at HIGH for 2 to 3
minutes, or until apple is tender, stirring after
every minute. Drain.

VEGETABLE FILLING

In small mixing bowl, combine ½ cup sliced
fresh mushrooms, ¼ cup chopped green
pepper, 2 tablespoons chopped onion and 1
tablespoon butter. Cover dish with plastic wrap.
Microwave at HIGH for 1½ to 2½ minutes, or
until green pepper and onion are tender.

CHEESY HAM AND POTATO FILLING

In small mixing bowl, combine 1 medium white
potato, baked (page 113), peeled and diced, and
½ cup diced fully-cooked ham. Just before
spooning onto omelet, microwave at POWER
LEVEL **9** for 1 minute, or until hot. After
spooning onto omelet, sprinkle with ½ cup
shredded Swiss cheese (about 2 oz.).

HAM AND EGG SCRAMBLE △

Power Level / HIGH
Approx. Cooking Time / 9 minutes
Yield / 4 to 6 servings

2 **tablespoons butter or margarine**
1 **tablespoon chopped onion**
8 **eggs**
⅓ **cup milk**
½ **teaspoon salt**
½ **teaspoon dried parsley flakes**
¼ **teaspoon dried rosemary leaves, crushed**
⅛ **teaspoon cayenne**
1 **cup cubed fully-cooked ham, ¼-inch cubes
   (about 6 oz.)**
1 **cup sliced fresh mushrooms**
1 **cup shredded Cheddar cheese (about 4 oz.)**

1 In 2-quart casserole, combine butter and
onion. Microwave at HIGH for 1¼ to 1½
minutes, or until butter melts.

2 Add eggs, milk, salt, parsley flakes, rosemary
and cayenne. Beat until well blended. Stir in
ham, mushrooms and half the Cheddar cheese.
Microwave at HIGH for 7 to 8 minutes, or until
eggs are set yet moist, stirring 2 or 3 times.

3 Sprinkle with remaining cheese. Cover. Let
stand for 4 to 5 minutes. Stir before serving.

QUICHE LORRAINE ▽

Power Level / **5**
Approx. Cooking Time / 29 minutes
Yield / 4 to 6 servings

  1 recipe Single Pie Crust, page 141
  1 cup half-and-half
  3 eggs
  2 tablespoons chopped green onion
  1 tablespoon all-purpose flour
1½ teaspoons freeze-dried chives
  ¼ teaspoon seasoned salt
  ¼ teaspoon white pepper
1½ cups shredded Swiss cheese (about 6 oz.)
  4 slices bacon, cooked and crumbled, page 63

1 Prepare and microwave crust as directed
   (follow directions in **TIP**). Set aside.

2 In small mixing bowl, combine half-and-half,
   eggs, onion, flour, chives, seasoned salt and
   white pepper. Beat until well blended. Microwave at POWER LEVEL **5** for 6 to 6½ minutes,
   or until hot yet not set, stirring 3 times.

3 Sprinkle cheese evenly into crust. Pour hot
   egg mixture over cheese. Sprinkle with bacon.
   Place quiche on saucer in oven. Microwave at
   POWER LEVEL **5** for 14 to 16 minutes, or
   until center is set yet moist, rotating plate
   every 5 minutes. Let stand for 5 minutes.

SPINACH PIE

Follow recipe above, adding 1 pkg. (10 oz.) frozen
chopped spinach, thawed and thoroughly
drained, to thickened egg mixture before pouring
into crust. Reduce Swiss cheese to 1 cup.

MACARONI AND CHEESE

Power Levels / HIGH, **7**, **8**
Approx. Cooking Time / 22 minutes
Yield / 4 to 6 servings

  1 tablespoon butter or margarine
  ¼ cup seasoned dry bread crumbs
  2 tablespoons butter or margarine
  2 tablespoons all-purpose flour
  ¾ teaspoon salt
  ¼ teaspoon pepper
1½ cups milk
1½ cups shredded Cheddar cheese (about 6 oz.)
  1 pkg. (7 oz.) elbow macaroni, cooked, page 122
  1 tablespoon finely-chopped onion

1 Place 1 tablespoon butter in small bowl.
   Microwave at HIGH for 45 to 60 seconds, or
   until butter melts. Stir in bread crumbs.
   Set aside.

2 Place 2 tablespoons butter in 1½-quart
   casserole. Microwave at HIGH for 45 to 60
   seconds, or until butter melts.

3 Stir flour, salt and pepper into butter. Blend in
   milk. Microwave at POWER LEVEL **7** for
   6 to 10 minutes, or until sauce thickens and
   bubbles, stirring once. Add Cheddar cheese.
   Stir until cheese melts. Stir in macaroni
   and onion.

4 Sprinkle with bread crumb mixture.
   Microwave at POWER LEVEL **8** for 8 to 10
   minutes, or until sauce bubbles and internal
   temperature registers 150°F.*

*Use temperature probe, if desired.

SWISS FONDUE ▷

Power Levels / HIGH, **7**
Approx. Cooking Time / 7 minutes
Yield / 2½ cups

¼ cup all-purpose flour
⅛ teaspoon garlic powder
⅛ teaspoon pepper
  Dash ground nutmeg
4 cups shredded Swiss cheese (about 1 lb.)
1 cup white wine or apple juice
2 tablespoons kirsch (optional)
  French bread cubes, about 1½-inch cubes

1 In large plastic food storage bag, mix flour, garlic powder, pepper and nutmeg. Add Swiss cheese. Shake to coat; set aside.

2 Pour wine into medium mixing bowl. Microwave at HIGH for 2 to 3 minutes, or until very hot yet not boiling.

3 Stir in cheese mixture and kirsch. Microwave at POWER LEVEL **7** for 3½ to 4½ minutes, or until mixture is heated through and can be stirred smooth, stirring 2 or 3 times. Serve with bread cubes.

WELSH RAREBIT

Power Levels / **8**, **7**
Approx. Cooking Time / 8 minutes
Yield / 4 to 6 servings

3 tablespoons all-purpose flour
½ teaspoon dry mustard
4 cups shredded Cheddar cheese (about 1 lb.)
⅔ cup beer
½ teaspoon Worcestershire sauce
  Toast points

1 In large plastic food storage bag, combine flour and mustard. Add Cheddar cheese. Shake to coat; set aside.

2 Pour beer into medium mixing bowl. Microwave at POWER LEVEL **8** for 2 to 3 minutes, or until very hot yet not boiling.

3 Stir in cheese mixture and Worcestershire sauce. Microwave at POWER LEVEL **7** for 4½ to 5½ minutes, or until mixture is heated through and can be stirred smooth, stirring after every minute. Serve over toast points.

BACON AND EGG RING

Power Levels / HIGH, **6**
Approx. Cooking Time / 23 minutes
Yield / 4 to 6 servings

¼ cup chopped onion
¼ cup chopped green pepper
1 tablespoon butter or margarine
6 slices bacon
8 eggs
¾ cup half-and-half
⅓ cup dairy sour cream
2 tablespoons snipped fresh parsley
2 tablespoons all-purpose flour
¼ teaspoon salt
¼ teaspoon dried marjoram or tarragon leaves
⅛ teaspoon pepper
1 cup shredded Cheddar cheese (about 4 oz.)

1 Lightly grease 9-inch ring dish. Set aside. In small bowl, combine onion, green pepper and butter. Cover bowl with plastic wrap. Microwave at HIGH for 1 to 1½ minutes, or until vegetables are tender-crisp.

2 Arrange bacon on roasting rack. Microwave at HIGH for 6 to 8 minutes, or until crisp. Crumble into medium mixing bowl. Add onion mixture, eggs, half-and-half, sour cream and parsley. Beat until well blended.

3 In large plastic food storage bag, mix flour, salt, marjoram and pepper. Add Cheddar cheese. Shake to coat. Stir into egg mixture.

4 Pour into prepared dish. Cover dish with plastic wrap. Microwave at POWER LEVEL **6** for 10 to 14 minutes, or until knife inserted in center comes out clean and no uncooked egg mixture remains on bottom of dish, rotating dish 2 times. Let stand for 5 minutes. Serve from dish or invert onto serving plate.

SAUCES

◁
MORNAY SAUCE

Power Levels / HIGH, **7**
Approx. Cooking Time / 7 minutes
Yield / 1½ cups

  2 tablespoons butter or margarine
  2 tablespoons all-purpose flour
1½ teaspoons dried parsley flakes
  1 cup chicken broth
⅓ cup half-and-half
⅓ cup shredded Swiss cheese (about 1⅓ oz.)
  2 tablespoons grated Parmesan cheese

1 Place butter in small mixing bowl. Microwave at HIGH for 45 to 60 seconds, or until
   butter melts.

2 Stir in flour and parsley flakes. Blend in broth
   and half-and-half. Microwave at HIGH for 3½
   to 4 minutes, or until sauce thickens and
   bubbles, stirring 2 times.

3 Stir in Swiss cheese and Parmesan cheese.
   Microwave at POWER LEVEL **7** for 1½ to 2
   minutes, or until cheeses melt, stirring once.
   Serve warm over vegetables or eggs.

LEMON SAUCE

Power Level / HIGH
Approx. Cooking Time / 5 minutes
Yield / About 1 cup

¾ cup water
⅓ cup sugar
¼ cup water
  1 tablespoon cornstarch
  2 tablespoons lemon juice
  1 tablespoon butter or margarine
  1 drop yellow food coloring

1 In 1-quart casserole, blend ¾ cup water and
   the sugar. Microwave at HIGH for 2 to 2½
   minutes, or until sugar dissolves,
   stirring once.

2 In small bowl, blend ¼ cup water and the
   cornstarch. Stir into sugar mixture. Stir in
   lemon juice. Microwave at HIGH for 2 to 2½
   minutes, or until mixture thickens, stirring
   once. Add butter and food coloring. Stir until
   butter melts. Serve warm over fruit or cake.

CUSTARD SAUCE

Power Levels / **7**, **5**
Approx. Cooking Time / 8 minutes
Yield / 2 cups

  3 tablespoons sugar
  2 tablespoons all-purpose flour
1½ cups milk
  2 egg yolks, slightly beaten
  1 teaspoon vanilla

1 In small mixing bowl, combine sugar and
   flour. Blend in milk. Microwave at POWER
   LEVEL **7** for 6½ to 7 minutes, or until sauce
   thickens and bubbles, stirring frequently.

2 Place egg yolks in small bowl. Blend small
   amount of hot mixture into egg yolks. Add
   back to hot mixture, stirring to combine.
   Microwave at POWER LEVEL **5** for 1 to 1½
   minutes, or until mixture thickens, stirring
   once. Stir in vanilla. Chill. Serve over fruit
   or cake.

LEMON CUSTARD SAUCE

Follow recipe above, substituting 1 tablespoon
lemon juice and 1 teaspoon grated lemon peel
for vanilla.

SWEET-AND-SOUR SAUCE

Power Level / HIGH
Approx. Cooking Time / 4 minutes
Yield / About 1½ cups

  1 can (8 oz.) crushed pineapple
    Water
¼ cup packed brown sugar
  2 tablespoons cider vinegar
  1 tablespoon soy sauce
  1 tablespoon chili sauce
  1 tablespoon cornstarch

1 Drain juice from crushed pineapple into 2-cup
   measure. Set pineapple aside. Add enough
   water to juice to make ¾ cup liquid.

2 Blend remaining ingredients except pineapple
   into liquid. Microwave at HIGH for 3 to 4
   minutes, or until bubbly and translucent,
   stirring once. Stir in pineapple. Serve with
   chicken, pork or shrimp.

◁

WHITE SAUCE

Power Level / HIGH
Approx. Cooking Time / 4 minutes
Yield / About 1 cup

THIN

1 tablespoon butter or margarine
1 tablespoon all-purpose flour
¼ teaspoon salt
⅛ teaspoon white pepper
1 cup milk

MEDIUM

2 tablespoons butter or margarine
2 tablespoons all-purpose flour
¼ teaspoon salt
⅛ teaspoon white pepper
1 cup milk

THICK

3 tablespoons butter or margarine
3 tablespoons all-purpose flour
¼ teaspoon salt
⅛ teaspoon white pepper
1 cup milk

1 Place butter in small mixing bowl. Microwave at HIGH for 45 to 60 seconds, or until butter melts.

2 Stir in flour, salt and white pepper. Blend in milk. Microwave at HIGH for 2½ to 3½ minutes, or until sauce thickens and bubbles, stirring after every minute.

CHEESE SAUCE

Follow recipe above, adding ½ cup shredded Cheddar or Colby cheese to thickened sauce. Stir until cheese melts.

CARAMEL SAUCE

Power Level / HIGH
Approx. Cooking Time / 4 minutes
Yield / 1½ cups

1 pkg. (14 oz.) caramels
¼ cup half-and-half
¼ teaspoon ground cinnamon

1 In small mixing bowl, combine all ingredients.

2 Microwave at HIGH for 3 to 4 minutes, or until caramels melt, stirring 2 times. Stir until smooth. Serve warm over ice cream or cake.

BRANDIED CHERRY SAUCE

Power Level / HIGH
Approx. Cooking Time / 4 minutes
Yield / About 2 cups

  1 can (17 oz.) pitted dark sweet cherries in heavy
     syrup
     Water
  1 tablespoon cornstarch
  ¼ cup brandy

1 Drain syrup from cherries into 1-cup measure.
   Set cherries aside. Add enough water to syrup
   to make 1 cup liquid. In small mixing bowl,
   blend liquid and cornstarch. Microwave at
   HIGH for about 3 minutes, or until thickened
   and translucent, stirring 1 or 2 times. Stir in
   cherries. Transfer sauce to serving dish.

2 Place brandy in small bowl. Microwave at
   HIGH for 30 to 45 seconds, or until hot yet not
   boiling. Pour over sauce. Carefully ignite.
   Serve immediately over ice cream or cake.

MELBA SAUCE

Power Level / HIGH
Approx. Cooking Time / 9 minutes
Yield / 2 cups

  1 pkg. (10 oz.) frozen sweetened raspberries
  1 can (16 oz.) peach slices
  ¼ cup water
  1 tablespoon plus 1½ teaspoons cornstarch

1 Place raspberries in shallow bowl. Microwave
   at HIGH for 2½ to 3½ minutes, stirring once to
   break apart. Let stand for 3 minutes. Drain,
   reserving juice. Set raspberries aside. Drain
   peach slices, reserving ½ cup juice. Set
   peaches aside.

2 In medium mixing bowl, blend water and
   cornstarch. Stir peach and raspberry juices
   into cornstarch mixture. Microwave at HIGH
   for 4 to 6 minutes, or until thickened and
   translucent, stirring 2 or 3 times. Cool. Stir in
   peaches and raspberries. Serve over ice cream
   or cake.

HOT FUDGE SAUCE ▽

Power Level / 5
Approx. Cooking Time / 2 minutes
Yield / 1½ cups

  1 pkg. (6 oz.) semisweet chocolate chips
  ½ cup light corn syrup
  ¼ cup half-and-half
  1 tablespoon butter or margarine
  1 teaspoon vanilla

1 In medium mixing bowl, combine chocolate
   chips and corn syrup. Microwave at POWER
   LEVEL 5 for 1½ to 2½ minutes, or until
   mixture can be stirred smooth.

2 Add remaining ingredients. Stir until butter
   melts and mixture is blended. Serve over ice
   cream or cake.

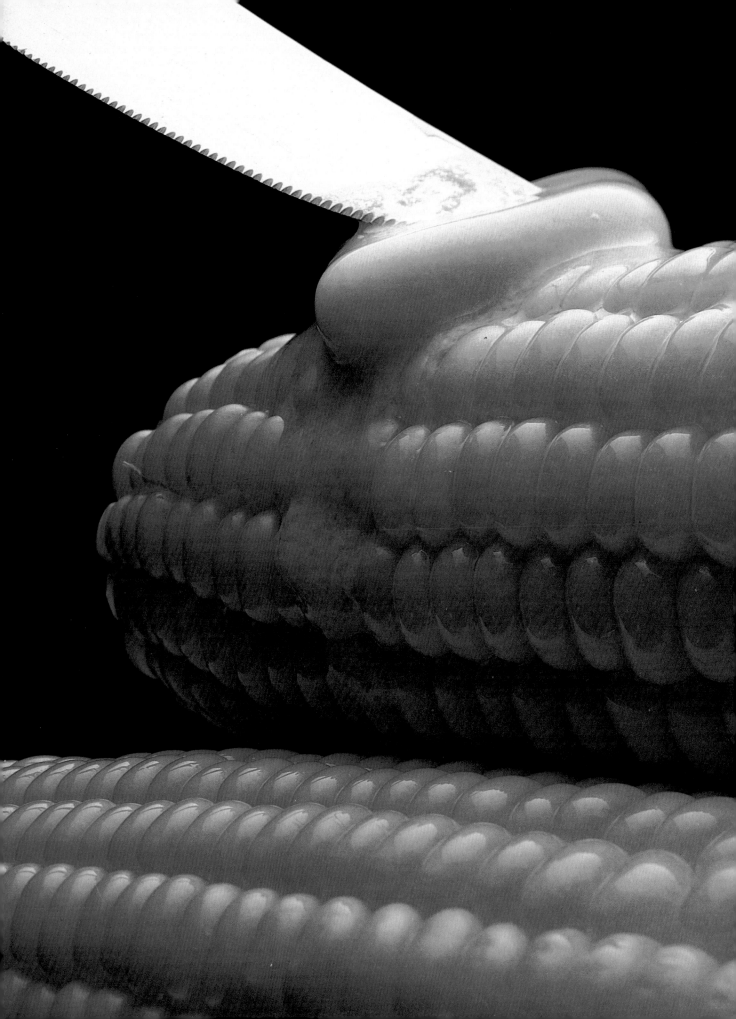

VEGETABLES

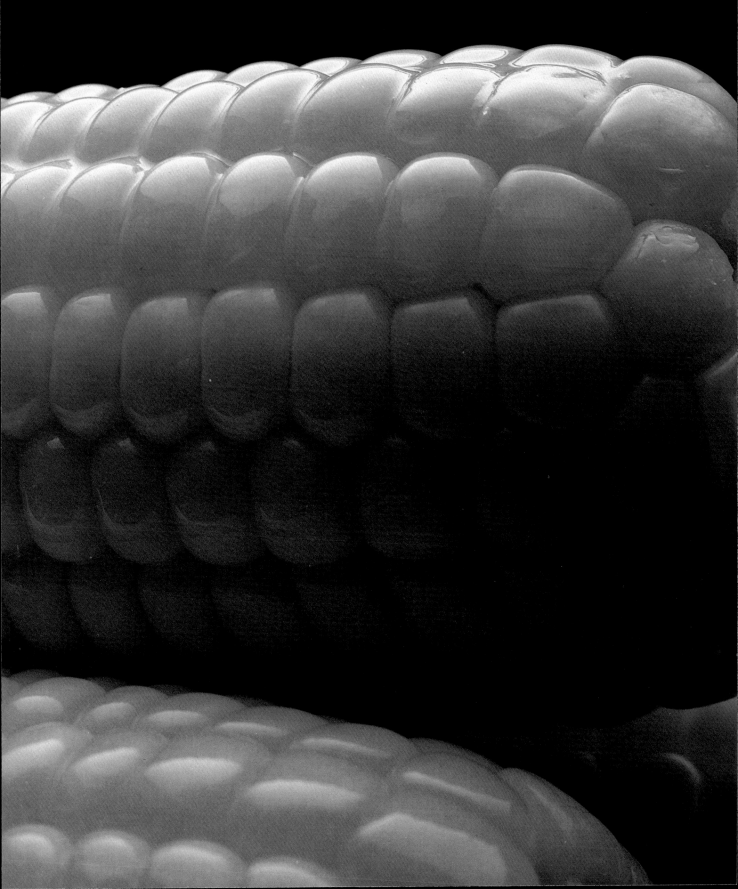

VEGETABLE COOKING GUIDE

ITEM	TOTAL COOKING TIME	POWER LEVEL	METHOD
Acorn Squash, 1 to 1½ lbs. each 1 2	6½ to 11½ min. 8 to 16 min.	HIGH	Pierce each squash at least once with knife. Microwave until tender, turning over once. Let stand for 5 min. Cut in half. Remove pulp and seeds.
Asparagus, fresh, 1 lb.	5½ to 8½ min.	HIGH	Arrange in 12 x 8-inch baking dish with tips toward center of dish. Add ¼ cup water. Cover dish with plastic wrap. Microwave until tender, rotating dish once. Let stand for 3 to 5 min.
Beans, green, fresh, 1 lb.	9 to 12 min.	HIGH	Trim and discard ends of beans. In 1½-quart casserole, combine beans and ¼ cup water. Cover. Microwave until tender, stirring once. Let stand for 3 to 5 min.
Beets, fresh, 1 lb.	15 to 20 min.	HIGH	Trim and discard leaves. In 1½-quart casserole, combine beets and ½ cup water. Cover. Microwave until tender, turning over once. Let stand for 3 to 5 min. Peel and trim ends of beets.
Broccoli Spears, fresh, 1 to 1½ lbs.	8 to 10 min.	HIGH	Trim and discard tough ends of spears. Arrange broccoli in 12 x 8-inch baking dish with flowers toward center of dish. Add ¼ cup water. Microwave until tender, rotating dish once. Let stand for 3 to 5 min.
Brussels Sprouts, fresh, 1 lb.	7 to 10 min.	HIGH	In 1½-quart casserole, combine sprouts and ¼ cup water. Cover. Microwave until tender, stirring once. Let stand for 3 to 5 min.
Cabbage chopped, 1½ lbs.	12 to 15 min.	HIGH	In 2-quart casserole, combine cabbage and 2 tablespoons water. Cover. Microwave until tender, stirring once. Let stand for 3 to 5 min.
wedges, 1 to 1½ lbs.	13 to 16 min.	HIGH	Arrange cabbage in 12 x 8-inch baking dish. Add ¼ cup water. Cover dish with plastic wrap. Microwave until tender, rearranging cabbage and rotating dish once. Let stand for 3 to 5 min.
Carrots, sliced, 2 cups	4 to 7 min.	HIGH	In 1-quart casserole, combine carrots and 2 tablespoons water. Cover. Microwave until tender, stirring once. Let stand for 3 to 5 min.
Cauliflower, fresh flowerets, 1½ lbs.	7 to 9 min.	HIGH	In 2-quart casserole, combine cauliflower and 2 tablespoons water. Cover. Microwave until tender, stirring 2 times. Let stand for 3 to 5 min.
whole 1 to 1½ lbs.	7 to 9 min.	HIGH	Trim and discard leaves and stem. Place cauliflower, cored-side up, on plate. Cover with plastic wrap. Microwave until tender, turning over after half the time. Let stand for 3 to 5 min.

Corn, on cob			
fresh, 7 to 8 oz. each			Husk corn. Arrange in baking dish. Add 2 tablespoons water. Cover dish with plastic wrap. Microwave until tender, turning over and rearranging once. Let stand for 3 to 5 min.
2	6 to 10 min	HIGH	
4	9 to 14 min.		
frozen			
large ears			Arrange in baking dish. Add 2 tablespoons water. Cover dish with plastic wrap. Microwave until tender, turning over and rearranging once. Let stand for 3 to 5 min.
2	7 to 9 min.	HIGH	
4	11 to 12 min.		
small ears			Same as above.
2	5 to 6 min.	HIGH	
4	7 to 8 min.		
Peas, green, fresh, shelled, 2 cups	5 to 7 min.	HIGH	In 1-quart casserole, combine peas and ¼ cup water. Cover. Microwave until tender, stirring once. Let stand for 3 to 5 min.
Potatoes			
white, 6 to 8 oz. each			Prick each potato several times with fork. Arrange at least 1 inch apart on paper towels. Microwave until tender.* Cover with inverted casserole, or wrap in aluminum foil. Let stand for 5 to 10 min.
1	3½ to 5½ min.	HIGH	
2	6 to 8 min.		
4	10½ to 12½ min.		
new, 1½ to 2 lbs.	6 to 9 min.	HIGH	Prick each potato several times with fork. In 2-quart casserole, combine potatoes and 3 tablespoons water. Cover. Microwave until tender, stirring once. Let stand for 3 to 5 min.
Spinach, fresh, 1 lb.	5 to 8 min.	HIGH	Wash and trim spinach. Place in 3-quart casserole. Cover. Microwave until tender, stirring once. Let stand for 2 to 3 min.
Sweet Potatoes or Yams, 5 to 7 oz. each			Prick each potato several times with fork. Arrange at least 1 inch apart on paper towels. Microwave until tender.* Let stand for 3 to 5 min.
1	3 to 6 min.	HIGH	
2	5 to 10 min.		
3	7 to 11 min.		
4	9 to 14 min.		
Zucchini, sliced, 1 lb.	6 to 8 min.	HIGH	In 2-quart casserole, combine zucchini and 2 tablespoons water. Cover. Microwave until tender, stirring 2 times. Let stand for 2 to 3 min.
Vegetables			
canned, 15 to 16 oz.	2 to 4 min.	HIGH	Drain vegetables, reserving 2 tablespoons liquid. In 1-quart casserole, combine vegetables and reserved liquid. Cover. Microwave until heated through, stirring once.
frozen, 8 to 12 oz.	5 to 8 min.	HIGH	In 1-quart casserole, combine vegetables and 2 tablespoons water. Cover. Microwave until heated through, stirring once. Let stand for 3 to 5 min.

*When microwaving 3 or 4 white potatoes, sweet potatoes or yams, turn them over and rearrange after half the time.

STUFFED ONIONS FLORENTINE ◁

Power Level / HIGH
Approx. Cooking Time / 20 minutes
Yield / 4 to 8 servings

  2 **very large onions (about 1 lb. each)**
  1 **pkg. (10 oz.) frozen chopped spinach**
  ¼ **lb. bulk pork sausage**
  ⅓ **cup shredded Cheddar cheese (about 1⅓ oz.)**
  ¼ **teaspoon salt**
    Dash pepper
    Dash ground nutmeg
  ¼ **cup hot water**

1 Make onion shells according to photo directions below.

2 Remove spinach from packaging and place on plate. Microwave at HIGH for 4 to 5 minutes. Let stand for 5 to 10 minutes. Press to remove excess moisture.

3 In 1-quart casserole, combine 1 tablespoon chopped onion and the sausage. Microwave at HIGH for 1½ to 2 minutes, or until sausage is no longer pink, stirring after half the time. Stir in remaining ingredients except hot water.

4 Arrange onion shells, cut-side up, in 9-inch round baking dish. Pour hot water around onions. Cover dish with plastic wrap. Microwave at HIGH for 5 minutes, rotating dish once.

5 Spoon an equal amount of spinach mixture into each onion shell. Re-cover. Microwave at HIGH for 7 to 8 minutes, or until onions are tender, rotating dish once. Let stand for 3 to 5 minutes.

HOW TO MAKE ONION SHELLS

CUT each onion in half lengthwise. With small knife, loosen center of each half to make a ½-inch thick shell.

REMOVE center of each half. Finely chop part of center portions to make 1 tablespoon; set aside. Refrigerate remaining onion for use in other recipes. Continue as directed in step 2 above.

SAVORY BEAN BAKE

Power Levels / HIGH, **5**
Approx. Cooking Time / 2 hours 18 minutes
Yield / 8 to 10 servings

1 pkg. (16 oz.) dried great northern beans, sorted,
   rinsed and drained
6 cups water
1 cup chopped onion
½ cup chopped green pepper
4 slices bacon, chopped
1 can (6 oz.) tomato paste
⅓ cup packed brown sugar
¼ cup dark corn syrup
1 teaspoon salt
½ teaspoon dry mustard
¼ teaspoon dried summer savory leaves
¼ teaspoon dried thyme leaves
⅛ teaspoon pepper

1 In 3-quart casserole, combine beans and
water. Cover. Microwave at HIGH for 9 to 11
minutes, or until water boils. Boil for 2
minutes. Let stand for 1 hour.

2 Stir in remaining ingredients. Re-cover. Microwave at HIGH for 5 minutes. Stir. Re-cover.

3 Reduce to POWER LEVEL **5**. Microwave for
1¾ to 2 hours longer, or until beans are tender,
stirring occasionally. Add water for thinner
sauce, if desired.

CRANBERRY SAUCE

Power Level / HIGH
Approx. Cooking Time / 12 minutes
Yield / 3 cups

2 cups sugar
¼ cup water
1 lb. frozen whole cranberries
2 tablespoons grated orange peel

1 In large mixing bowl, combine sugar and
water. Microwave at HIGH for 3 to 4 minutes,
or until sugar dissolves, stirring once.

2 Add cranberries. Cover. Microwave at HIGH
for 6 to 8 minutes, or until cranberries soften,
stirring 3 or 4 times. Stir in orange peel. Mash
berries with fork. Serve warm or chilled.

RATATOUILLE △

Power Level / HIGH
Approx. Cooking Time / 17 minutes
Yield / 6 to 8 servings

1 medium onion, thinly sliced
1 medium green pepper, cored, seeded and thinly
   sliced into rings
3 tablespoons vegetable oil
2 cloves garlic, minced
1 medium eggplant, peeled and cut into ½-inch
   cubes
2 medium zucchini, thinly sliced
2 medium tomatoes, seeded and chopped
½ cup tomato juice or vegetable juice cocktail
1 teaspoon dried basil leaves
1 teaspoon dried parsley flakes
½ teaspoon salt
¼ teaspoon pepper
2 tablespoons grated Parmesan cheese

1 In 5-quart casserole, combine onion, green
pepper, oil and garlic. Cover. Microwave at
HIGH for 8 to 10 minutes, or until vegetables
are tender, stirring 2 or 3 times.

2 Stir in remaining ingredients except Parmesan
cheese. Re-cover. Microwave at HIGH for 5 to
7 minutes, or until zucchini is tender and
flavors are blended, stirring 2 or 3 times.
Sprinkle with Parmesan cheese.

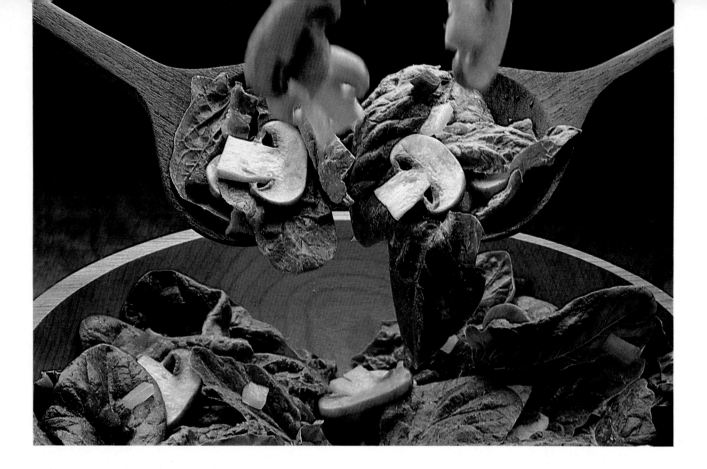

WILTED SPINACH SALAD △

Power Level / HIGH
Approx. Cooking Time / 4 minutes
Yield / 4 servings

½ lb. fresh spinach, rinsed and trimmed
1 cup sliced fresh mushrooms
2 tablespoons chopped pimiento
3 slices bacon, chopped
1 tablespoon plus 2 teaspoons finely-chopped
    onion
3 tablespoons water
3 tablespoons cider vinegar
1 tablespoon sugar
  Dash cayenne

1 In serving bowl, combine spinach,
  mushrooms and pimiento. Set aside.

2 In 1-quart casserole, combine bacon and
  onion. Microwave at HIGH for 2½ to 3½
  minutes, or until bacon is brown, stirring 1 or
  2 times.

3 Stir remaining ingredients into bacon mixture.
  Microwave at HIGH for 30 to 60 seconds, or
  until mixture boils. Pour over spinach mixture.
  Toss to coat. Serve immediately.

GERMAN POTATO SALAD

Power Level / HIGH
Approx. Cooking Time / 8 minutes
Yield / 6 to 8 servings

4 slices bacon, chopped
¼ cup chopped onion
⅓ cup cider vinegar
1 tablespoon plus 1½ teaspoons packed brown
    sugar
2 teaspoons all-purpose flour
¼ teaspoon celery seed
¼ teaspoon salt
⅛ teaspoon pepper
4 white potatoes, baked, page 113

1 In 2-quart casserole, combine bacon and
  onion. Microwave at HIGH for 4 to 5 minutes,
  or until bacon is brown.

2 Stir in remaining ingredients except potatoes.
  Microwave at HIGH for 1 to 1½ minutes, or
  until mixture is bubbly, stirring 1 or 2 times.

3 Peel and thinly slice baked potatoes. Gently
  stir into bacon mixture. Cover. Microwave
  at HIGH for 1 to 2 minutes, or until
  heated through.

TWICE-BAKED POTATOES ▷

Power Level / HIGH
Approx. Cooking Time / 19 minutes
Yield / 4 servings

 4 medium white potatoes, baked, page 113
½ cup shredded Cheddar cheese (about 2 oz.)
⅓ cup milk
 1 egg
 2 tablespoons butter or margarine
½ teaspoon salt
¼ teaspoon pepper
   Paprika

1 Make potato shells according to photo
  directions below.

2 In medium mixing bowl, combine scooped-
  out potato, Cheddar cheese, milk, egg, butter,
  salt and pepper. Beat at medium speed of
  electric mixer until smooth.

3 Spoon an equal amount of potato mixture into
  each potato shell. Sprinkle with paprika.
  Arrange on baking sheet. Microwave at HIGH
  for 5½ to 6½ minutes, or until potatoes are
  heated through, rotating baking sheet once.

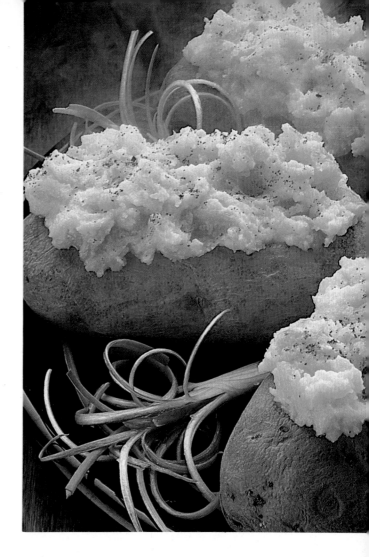

HOW TO MAKE POTATO SHELLS

CUT a thin lengthwise strip from top of
each potato.

SCOOP out center of each potato, leaving a
¼-inch thick shell, reserving scooped-out potato.
Continue as directed in step 2 above.

BAKED HERB TOMATOES

Power Level / HIGH
Approx. Cooking Time / 6 minutes
Yield / 4 servings

2 medium tomatoes, cut in half
2 tablespoons butter or margarine
3 tablespoons seasoned dry bread crumbs
2 tablespoons grated Parmesan cheese
½ teaspoon dried basil or oregano leaves

1 Arrange tomatoes, cut-side up, in 9-inch pie plate. Set aside. Place butter in small bowl. Microwave at HIGH for 45 to 60 seconds, or until butter melts. Stir in remaining ingredients.

2 Spoon an equal amount of crumb mixture onto each tomato half. Microwave at HIGH for 3 to 5 minutes, or until heated through, rotating plate once.

GREEN BEANS AMANDINE

Power Level / HIGH
Approx. Cooking Time / 14 minutes
Yield / 4 to 6 servings

1 lb. fresh green beans, trimmed
¼ cup water
2 tablespoons butter or margarine
¼ cup slivered almonds
½ teaspoon salt

1 In 2-quart casserole, combine beans and water. Cover. Microwave at HIGH for 8 to 10 minutes, or until beans are tender, stirring once. Drain. Re-cover. Set aside.

2 Place butter in small bowl. Microwave at HIGH for 45 to 60 seconds, or until butter melts.

3 Stir almonds into melted butter. Microwave at HIGH for 2½ to 3½ minutes, or until almonds begin to brown, stirring after every minute. Stir almonds and salt into beans.

SWISS SCALLOPED CORN

Power Levels / HIGH, **5**
Approx. Cooking Time / 20 minutes
Yield / 6 to 8 servings

1 tablespoon butter or margarine
¼ cup unseasoned dry bread crumbs
  Dash paprika
3 slices bacon
2 cans (16 oz. each) whole kernel corn, drained
1 cup shredded Swiss cheese (about 4 oz.)
1 can (5⅓ oz.) evaporated milk
1 egg
1 tablespoon all-purpose flour
½ teaspoon onion powder
⅛ teaspoon pepper

1 Place butter in small bowl. Microwave at HIGH for 45 to 60 seconds, or until butter melts. Stir in bread crumbs and paprika. Set aside.

2 Arrange bacon on roasting rack. Cover with paper towel. Microwave at HIGH for 2½ to 3 minutes, or until bacon is crisp. Crumble into 1½-quart casserole. Stir in corn and Swiss cheese.

3 In small mixing bowl, blend remaining ingredients. Stir into corn mixture. Microwave at POWER LEVEL **5** for 12 to 14 minutes, or until cheese melts, stirring occasionally.

4 Sprinkle with bread crumb mixture. Microwave at POWER LEVEL **5** for 2 minutes, or until hot.

SAUTÉED MUSHROOMS

Power Level / HIGH
Approx. Cooking Time / 9 minutes
Yield / 4 to 6 servings

1 lb. fresh mushrooms, sliced
¼ cup butter or margarine
⅛ teaspoon garlic powder

1 In 1½-quart casserole, combine all ingredients. Cover dish with wax paper.

2 Microwave at HIGH for 6 to 9 minutes, or until mushrooms are tender, stirring 1 or 2 times.

SPICED SWEET POTATO BAKE

Power Levels / **8**, HIGH
Approx. Cooking Time / 16 minutes
Yield / 6 to 8 servings

  2 cans (23 oz. each) sweet potatoes, drained
  2 eggs
  3 tablespoons packed brown sugar
  2 tablespoons light molasses
  2 teaspoons grated orange peel
  1 teaspoon ground cinnamon
  ½ teaspoon ground nutmeg
  ⅛ teaspoon ground cloves
  ⅓ cup chopped pecans
  ¾ cup miniature marshmallows
  ½ teaspoon ground cinnamon

1 In medium mixing bowl, combine sweet
  potatoes, eggs, brown sugar, molasses, orange
  peel, 1 teaspoon cinnamon, the nutmeg and
  cloves. Beat at low speed of electric mixer until
  smooth. Stir in pecans.

2 Transfer sweet potato mixture to 1½-quart
  casserole. Cover dish with wax paper.
  Microwave at POWER LEVEL **8** for 13 to 15
  minutes, or until knife inserted in center
  comes out clean, stirring every 5 minutes.

3 In small plastic food storage bag, combine
  marshmallows and ½ teaspoon cinnamon.
  Shake to coat marshmallows. Sprinkle mixture
  over casserole. Microwave at HIGH for 45
  seconds to 1¼ minutes, or until marshmallows
  are puffy, rotating casserole once.

GLAZED CARROT COINS

Power Level / HIGH
Approx. Cooking Time / 7 minutes
Yield / 4 to 6 servings

  2 cups thinly-sliced carrots
  2 tablespoons orange juice
  3 tablespoons packed brown sugar
  1 tablespoon butter or margarine
  ¼ teaspoon grated lemon peel

1 In 1-quart casserole, combine carrots and
  orange juice. Cover. Microwave at HIGH for
  3 minutes.

2 Stir in remaining ingredients. Re-cover.
  Microwave at HIGH for 2 to 4 minutes, or until
  carrots are tender-crisp. Let stand for 2 minutes.

ITALIAN ZUCCHINI △

Power Level / HIGH
Approx. Cooking Time / 9 minutes
Yield / 4 to 6 servings

  ½ teaspoon dried basil leaves
  ½ teaspoon dried marjoram leaves
  ¼ teaspoon dried oregano leaves
  3 medium zucchini, cut into ¼-inch slices
  2 tablespoons butter or margarine

1 In small bowl, mix basil, marjoram and
  oregano. Set aside. Arrange half of zucchini in
  1½-quart casserole. Sprinkle with half of herb
  mixture. Dot with half of butter. Repeat with
  remaining zucchini, herb mixture and
  butter. Cover.

2 Microwave at HIGH for 7 to 9 minutes, or
  until zucchini is tender-crisp. Let stand for
  3 minutes.

PASTAS, CEREALS & GRAINS

PASTA AND RICE COOKING GUIDE

ITEM	HOT WATER	VEGETABLE OIL	SALT	TOTAL COOKING TIME	POWER LEVEL	METHOD
Egg Noodles, 3 cups Yield: 3 cups	6 cups	1 Tbsp.	1 tsp.	25 min.	HIGH	In 3-quart casserole, combine water, oil and salt. Cover. Microwave for 10 to 15 min., or until boiling. Stir. Add noodles. Stir. Microwave for 8 to 10 min., or until tender, stirring once. Rinse and drain.
Elbow Macaroni, 7 oz. Yield: 4 cups	6 cups	1 Tbsp.	1 tsp.	23 min.	HIGH	In 3-quart casserole, combine water, oil and salt. Cover. Microwave for 10 to 15 min., or until boiling. Stir. Add macaroni. Stir. Microwave for 6 to 8 min., or until tender, stirring once. Rinse and drain.
Small Shell Macaroni, ¾ to 1 cup Yield: 1½ to 2 cups	6 cups	1 Tbsp.	1 tsp.	23 min.	HIGH	Same as above.
Spaghetti, 7 to 8 oz. Yield: 4 cups	6 cups	1 Tbsp.	1 tsp.	26 min.	HIGH	In 3-quart casserole, combine water, oil and salt. Cover. Microwave for 10 to 15 min., or until boiling. Stir. Add spaghetti. Stir. Microwave for 9 to 11 min., or until tender, stirring once. Rinse and drain.
Rice, long grain, 1 cup Yield: 3 cups	2 cups		1 tsp.	22 min.	HIGH for first 5 min. of total time, then **5** for 15 to 17 min.	In 2-quart casserole, combine rice, water, salt and 2 teaspoons butter or margarine. Cover. Microwave until rice is tender and liquid is absorbed. Let stand for 5 min. Fluff with fork.

CITRUS NOODLES

Power Levels / HIGH, **8**
Approx. Cooking Time / 2 minutes
Yield / 4 servings

¼ **cup butter or margarine**
½ **cup sliced almonds**
 1 **tablespoon poppy seed**
½ **teaspoon grated lemon peel**
½ **teaspoon grated orange peel**
½ **teaspoon salt**
⅛ **teaspoon pepper**
 3 **cups narrow egg noodles, cooked, above**

1 Place butter in 1½-quart casserole. Microwave at HIGH for 45 seconds to 1¼ minutes, or until butter melts.

2 Stir in remaining ingredients except noodles. Add noodles. Toss to coat. Microwave at POWER LEVEL **8** for 1 minute, or until hot.

NOODLES ALFREDO

Power Levels / HIGH, **8**
Approx. Cooking Time / 4 minutes
Yield / 4 to 6 servings

 1 **cup grated Parmesan cheese**
½ **cup butter or margarine, cut into chunks**
½ **cup whipping cream**
 1 **tablespoon snipped fresh parsley**
 3 **cups egg noodles, cooked, above**

1 In 1-quart casserole, combine Parmesan cheese, butter, whipping cream and parsley. Microwave at HIGH for 2 to 3 minutes, or until butter melts, stirring 2 or 3 times.

2 Add noodles. Stir to coat. Microwave at POWER LEVEL **8** for 1 minute, or until hot.

HOPPIN' JOHN △

Power Levels / HIGH, **5**
Approx. Cooking Time / 37 minutes
Yield / 6 servings

  1 medium onion, chopped
  4 slices bacon, chopped
2½ cups hot water
  1 can (15 oz.) black-eyed peas, drained
  1 cup uncooked long grain rice
  1 teaspoon salt
 ¼ teaspoon pepper
   Dash hot pepper sauce

1 In 2-quart casserole, combine onion and bacon. Microwave at HIGH for 5 to 6 minutes, or until bacon is crisp, stirring 2 times.

2 Stir in remaining ingredients. Cover. Microwave at HIGH for 5 to 6 minutes, or until mixture boils.

3 Reduce to POWER LEVEL **5**. Microwave for 20 to 25 minutes longer, or until liquid is absorbed and rice is tender. Let stand for 5 minutes.

HOT PASTA SALAD △

Power Level / **8**
Approx. Cooking Time / 11 minutes
Yield / 6 to 8 servings

  1 cup thinly-sliced carrot
 ¾ cup small shell macaroni, cooked, page 122
  1 medium green pepper, cored, seeded and cut into ½-inch strips
  1 small onion, cut in half lengthwise, thinly sliced
 ½ cup thinly-sliced celery, cut on diagonal
  1 tablespoon olive oil
  1 clove garlic, minced
 ½ teaspoon salt
 ¼ teaspoon dried oregano leaves
 ⅛ teaspoon pepper
   Dash dried basil leaves
   Dash dried thyme leaves
   Dash dried rosemary leaves
  1 large tomato, seeded and chopped

1 In 1½-quart casserole, combine all ingredients except tomato. Mix well. Cover. Microwave at POWER LEVEL **8** for 5 to 7 minutes, or until green pepper is tender-crisp.

2 Stir in tomato. Re-cover. Microwave at POWER LEVEL **8** for 3 to 4 minutes, or until heated through, stirring once.

CEREAL COOKING GUIDE

ITEM/ SERVINGS	BOWL SIZE	CEREAL	SALT	HOT WATER	TOTAL COOKING TIME AT HIGH	METHOD
Farina						
quick						
1	1 qt.	2½ Tbsp.	⅛ tsp.	¾ cup	1½ to 2½ min.	In bowl, combine cereal and salt. Stir
2	2 qt.	⅓ cup	¼ tsp.	1⅓ cups	2½ to 3½ min.	in water. Microwave, stirring once.
4	3 qt.	⅔ cup	½ tsp.	3½ cups	5 to 6 min.	Stir before serving.
regular						
1	1 qt.	2½ Tbsp.	⅛ tsp.	1 cup	4 to 6 min.	Same as above.
2	2 qt.	⅓ cup	¼ tsp.	1¾ cups	5½ to 7½ min.	
4	3 qt.	⅔ cup	½ tsp.	3½ cups	9 to 12 min.	
Grits						
quick						
2	2 qt.	6 Tbsp.	¼ tsp.	1½ cups	3 to 3½ min.	In bowl, combine grits and salt. Stir in
4	3 qt.	¾ cup	¼ tsp.	3 cups	5 to 6 min.	water. Microwave, stirring 2 or 3 times. Stir before serving.
Oats						
quick						
1	1 qt.	⅓ cup	¼ tsp.	¾ cup	2 to 2½ min.	In bowl, combine oats and salt. Stir in
2	1½ qt.	⅔ cup	½ tsp.	1½ cups	4 to 5 min.	water. Microwave, stirring once. Stir
4	2 qt.	1⅓ cups	¾ tsp.	3 cups	6 to 7 min.	before serving.
regular						
1	1 qt.	⅓ cup	⅛ tsp.	1 cup	3 to 3½ min.	In bowl, combine oats and salt. Stir in
2	2 qt.	⅔ cup	¼ tsp.	1½ cups	4½ to 6½ min.	water. Microwave, stirring after first
4	3 qt.	1⅓ cups	½ tsp.	3 cups	7 to 9 min.	2 minutes, then 1 or 2 times. Stir before serving.

CINNAMON RAISIN OATMEAL

Power Level / HIGH
Approx. Cooking Time / 6 minutes
Yield / 6 to 8 servings

4 cups hot water
2 cups quick-cooking rolled oats
½ cup raisins
¼ cup packed brown sugar
¼ teaspoon salt
1 teaspoon ground cinnamon

1 In 2-quart casserole, mix all ingredients except cinnamon. Microwave at HIGH for 4 to 6 minutes, or until mixture slightly thickens.

2 Stir in cinnamon. Let stand for 1 to 2 minutes.

CINNAMON APRICOT OATMEAL

Follow recipe above, substituting chopped dried apricots for raisins.

CRUNCHY GRANOLA

Power Level / HIGH
Approx. Cooking Time / 5 minutes
Yield / 4 cups

2 cups rolled oats
⅔ cup chopped nuts
⅓ cup wheat germ
¼ cup packed brown sugar
¼ cup honey
1 teaspoon vanilla
⅓ cup raisins or flaked coconut

1 In 12 x 8-inch baking dish, mix oats, nuts, wheat germ and brown sugar. In small bowl, blend honey and vanilla. Pour over oat mixture. Stir to coat.

2 Microwave at HIGH for 3 to 5 minutes, or until hot, stirring 2 or 3 times. Stir in raisins. Cool completely. Store in covered container.

BARLEY MUSHROOM CASSEROLE △

Power Levels / HIGH, **5**
Approx. Cooking Time / 29 minutes
Yield / 8 to 10 servings

⅔ cup finely-chopped onion
6 tablespoons butter or margarine
1 clove garlic, minced
1 lb. fresh mushrooms, sliced
1⅓ cups water
1 cup quick-cooking barley
¼ cup snipped fresh parsley
1 teaspoon instant chicken bouillon granules
1 teaspoon dried basil leaves
½ teaspoon salt
¼ teaspoon pepper

1 In 2-quart casserole, combine onion, butter and garlic. Cover. Microwave at HIGH for 4 to 4½ minutes, or until onion is tender.

2 Stir in remaining ingredients. Re-cover. Microwave at HIGH for 5 minutes. Stir. Re-cover.

3 Reduce to POWER LEVEL **5**. Microwave for about 20 minutes longer, or until barley is tender and liquid is absorbed, stirring occasionally. Let stand for 5 minutes.

CHERRY BREAKFAST RING

Power Levels / HIGH, **7**
Approx. Cooking Time / 6 minutes
Yield / 4 to 6 servings

3 tablespoons butter or margarine
¼ cup packed brown sugar
1 tablespoon half-and-half
⅓ cup chopped maraschino cherries
¼ cup flaked coconut
1 pkg. (7½ oz.) refrigerated buttermilk biscuits
2 teaspoons granulated sugar
1 teaspoon ground cinnamon

1 Place butter in small mixing bowl. Microwave at HIGH for 45 to 60 seconds, or until butter melts. Stir in brown sugar and half-and-half. Microwave at HIGH for 1 minute, stirring once.

2 Place a small drinking glass, right side up, in center of ungreased 9-inch round baking dish. Spread brown sugar mixture evenly around glass. Sprinkle with cherries and coconut. Arrange biscuits on top.

3 In small bowl, mix granulated sugar and cinnamon. Sprinkle evenly over biscuits. Microwave at POWER LEVEL **7** for 3½ to 4½ minutes, or until biscuits spring back when touched lightly, rotating dish 1 or 2 times. Let stand for 2 to 3 minutes. Remove glass. Invert onto serving plate.

HOW TO SHIELD LOAF DISH

SHIELD loaf dish by placing a 2-inch wide strip of aluminum foil at each end of dish, covering about 1 inch of batter and molding remainder around handle of dish.

NUT BREAD

Power Levels / HIGH, **5**
Approx. Cooking Time / 15 minutes
Yield / 1 loaf

1 tablespoon graham cracker crumbs
1¼ cups all-purpose flour
½ cup packed brown sugar
¼ cup granulated sugar
1½ teaspoons baking powder
½ teaspoon salt
½ teaspoon ground cinnamon
½ cup butter or margarine
¾ cup chopped nuts
⅔ cup buttermilk
2 eggs, slightly beaten
½ teaspoon vanilla

1 Grease bottom and sides of 8 x 4-inch loaf dish. Line bottom of dish with wax paper. Grease wax paper. Sprinkle with graham cracker crumbs. Tilt dish to coat sides and bottom. Shake out and discard excess crumbs. Set dish aside.

2 In medium mixing bowl, mix flour, brown sugar, granulated sugar, baking powder, salt and cinnamon. Set aside. Place butter in small bowl. Microwave at HIGH for 15 to 30 seconds, or until butter softens.

3 Add softened butter and remaining ingredients to flour mixture. Beat at low speed of electric mixer until dry ingredients are moistened, scraping bowl constantly. Beat at medium speed for 2 minutes, scraping bowl occasionally. Pour into prepared dish. Shield ends of dish with aluminum foil (left).

4 Place dish on saucer in oven. Microwave at POWER LEVEL **5** for 9 minutes, rotating dish 2 or 3 times.

5 Increase power to HIGH. Microwave for 2 minutes. Remove foil. Microwave at HIGH for 2 to 4 minutes longer, or until wooden pick inserted in center comes out clean. Let stand for 5 to 10 minutes.

BLUEBERRY NUT BREAD

Follow recipe above, folding ½ cup blueberries into batter before pouring into loaf dish.

RAISIN NUT BREAD

Follow recipe above, folding ½ cup raisins into batter before pouring into loaf dish.

CRANBERRY ORANGE COFFEE RING ▷

Power Levels / HIGH, **5**
Approx. Cooking Time / 10 minutes
Yield / 6 to 8 servings

 1 tablespoon butter or margarine
 1 can (8 oz.) whole berry cranberry sauce
 ¼ cup granulated sugar
 ¼ cup chopped walnuts (optional)
 1½ cups buttermilk baking mix
 ¾ cup orange juice
 1 egg, slightly beaten
 2 tablespoons granulated sugar
 ½ cup powdered sugar
 ¼ teaspoon vanilla
 2 to 3 teaspoons water

1 Line bottom of 9-inch round baking dish with wax paper. Place a small drinking glass, right side up, in center of dish. Set aside.

2 Place butter in small mixing bowl. Microwave at HIGH for 45 to 60 seconds, or until butter melts. Stir in cranberry sauce, ¼ cup granulated sugar and the walnuts. Spread mixture evenly around glass in baking dish.

3 In medium mixing bowl, combine baking mix, orange juice, egg and 2 tablespoons granulated sugar. Stir until well mixed. Spread over cranberry mixture. Place dish on saucer in oven. Microwave at POWER LEVEL **5** for 6 minutes, rotating dish once.

4 Rotate dish again. Increase power to HIGH. Microwave for 2½ to 3½ minutes longer, or until cake springs back when touched lightly. Let stand for 5 minutes. Invert onto serving plate. Cool slightly.

5 In small bowl, mix powdered sugar and vanilla. Stir in enough water to make desired consistency. Drizzle over cake.

BANANA NUT COFFEE CAKE

Power Levels / **5**, HIGH
Approx. Cooking Time / 12 minutes
Yield / 6 to 8 servings

CAKE
 ½ cup mashed ripe banana (about 1 medium)
 ½ cup packed brown sugar
 ¼ cup vegetable oil
 ¼ cup milk
 1 egg, slightly beaten
 1 cup all-purpose flour
 ½ cup chopped nuts
 ¾ teaspoon baking powder
 ½ teaspoon salt
 ¼ teaspoon baking soda

TOPPING
 ¼ cup packed brown sugar
 ¼ cup chopped nuts
 2 tablespoons all-purpose flour
 ¼ teaspoon ground cinnamon
 1 tablespoon butter or margarine

1 For cake, in medium mixing bowl, blend banana, brown sugar, oil, milk and egg. Add remaining cake ingredients. Stir just until dry ingredients are moistened. Pour into ungreased 9-inch round baking dish. Place on saucer in oven. Microwave at POWER LEVEL **5** for 6 minutes, rotating dish once.

2 For topping, in small mixing bowl, mix all ingredients except butter. Cut butter into dry ingredients until mixture is crumbly. Sprinkle on cake. Microwave at HIGH for 4 to 6 minutes, or until center springs back when touched lightly. Let stand for 5 to 10 minutes.

CHILI CHEESE CORNBREAD △

Power Levels / HIGH, **7**
Approx. Cooking Time / 11 minutes
Yield / 4 to 6 servings

½ cup all-purpose flour
½ cup yellow cornmeal
1½ teaspoons baking powder
½ teaspoon salt
2 tablespoons butter or margarine
¾ cup shredded Cheddar cheese (about 3 oz.)
½ cup dairy sour cream
½ cup whole kernel corn
1 egg, slightly beaten
2 tablespoons chopped green chilies
   Dash hot pepper sauce
   Dash pepper

1 In medium mixing bowl, mix flour, cornmeal, baking powder and salt. Set aside. Place butter in small bowl. Microwave at HIGH for 45 to 60 seconds, or until butter melts. Add butter and remaining ingredients to flour mixture. Stir just until dry ingredients are moistened.

2 Spread in ungreased 9-inch round baking dish. Place on saucer in oven. Microwave at POWER LEVEL **7** for 8 to 10 minutes, or until center springs back when touched lightly, rotating dish once. Let stand for 3 to 5 minutes. Serve warm.

PUMPKIN MUFFINS

Power Level / HIGH
Approx. Cooking Time / 6 minutes
Yield / 1 dozen muffins

1 cup all-purpose flour
⅔ cup sugar
½ cup canned pumpkin
½ cup raisins
½ cup chopped pecans or walnuts
¼ cup milk
1 egg, slightly beaten
3 tablespoons vegetable oil
1 to 1½ teaspoons pumpkin pie spice
1 teaspoon baking powder
⅛ teaspoon salt

1 Line 6 muffin cups with paper liners. Set aside. In medium mixing bowl, combine all ingredients. Stir just until dry ingredients are moistened.

2 Divide half of batter evenly among muffin cups, filling each cup half to two-thirds full of batter. Microwave at HIGH for 2 to 3 minutes, or until muffins are almost dry on top, rotating cups 1 or 2 times. Let stand for 2 to 3 minutes. Remove muffins from cups. Re-line muffin cups. Repeat with remaining batter.

BREAKFAST SPICE MUFFINS ▽

Power Level / HIGH
Approx. Cooking Time / 7 minutes
Yield / 1 dozen muffins

MUFFINS

1¾ cups all-purpose flour
½ cup sugar
½ cup milk
½ cup vegetable oil
2 eggs, slightly beaten
1 tablespoon baking powder
1½ teaspoons vanilla
½ teaspoon salt

TOPPING

¼ cup butter or margarine
2 tablespoons plus 1 teaspoon sugar
2 teaspoons ground nutmeg
¼ teaspoon ground ginger
⅛ teaspoon ground allspice

1 Line 6 muffin cups with paper liners. Set aside. For muffins, in medium mixing bowl, combine all ingredients. Stir just until dry ingredients are moistened.

2 Divide half of batter evenly among muffin cups, filling each cup half to two-thirds full of batter. Microwave at HIGH for 2 to 3 minutes, or until muffins are almost dry on top, rotating cups 1 or 2 times. Let stand for 2 to 3 minutes. Remove muffins from cups. Re-line muffin cups. Repeat with remaining batter.

3 For topping, place ¼ cup butter in small bowl. Microwave at HIGH for 45 seconds to 1¼ minutes, or until butter melts. In another small bowl, mix remaining topping ingredients. Dip tops of muffins in butter, then in sugar mixture to coat.

POPPY SEED COFFEE CAKE

Power Levels / HIGH, **5**
Approx. Cooking Time / 11 minutes
Yield / 6 to 8 servings

1 tablespoon butter or margarine
¼ cup graham cracker crumbs
½ cup butter or margarine
1¼ cups all-purpose flour
⅓ cup packed brown sugar
1 egg
½ cup milk
3 tablespoons poppy seed
1½ teaspoons vanilla
1¼ teaspoons baking powder
½ teaspoon salt

1 Place 1 tablespoon butter in small bowl. Microwave at HIGH for 45 to 60 seconds, or until butter melts. Stir in graham cracker crumbs. Set aside.

2 Place ½ cup butter in medium mixing bowl. Microwave at HIGH for 15 to 30 seconds, or until butter softens. Add flour, brown sugar and egg. Cream at high speed of electric mixer. Add remaining ingredients. Beat at medium speed until blended, scraping bowl occasionally.

3 Spread in ungreased 9-inch round baking dish. Place on saucer in oven. Microwave at POWER LEVEL **5** for 6 minutes, rotating dish 1 or 2 times.

4 Sprinkle cracker crumb mixture on cake. Microwave at HIGH for 2½ to 3½ minutes, or until center springs back when touched lightly, rotating dish once. Let stand for 5 to 10 minutes.

DESSERTS

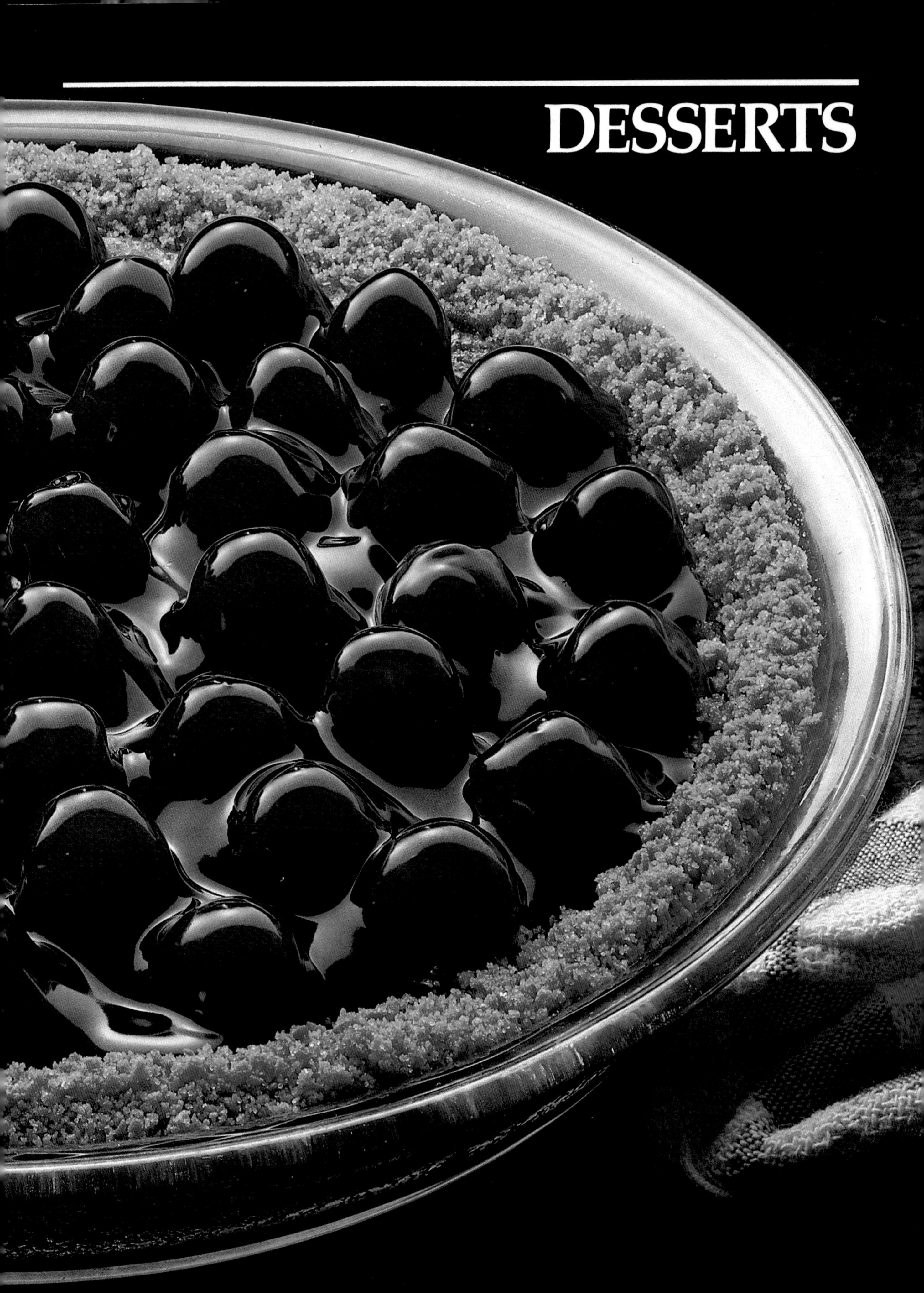

DESSERT COOKING GUIDE

ITEM	TOTAL COOKING TIME	POWER LEVEL	METHOD
Ring Cake, fluted, 10 to 12 cup	11½ to 13 min.	**5** for first 8 min., then HIGH for 3½ to 5 min.	Place dish on saucer in oven. Microwave until edges begin to pull away from sides and knife inserted in center comes out clean, rotating dish 3 or 4 times. Let stand for 10 min. Invert onto serving plate.
Cake Layer, 9 inch round	9 to 11 min.	**5** for first 6 min., then HIGH for 3 to 5 min.	Microwave until edges begin to pull away from sides and center springs back when touched lightly, rotating dish 1 or 2 times. Let stand for 5 to 10 min. Invert onto serving plate.
Cupcakes or Muffins, up to 6 at a time	20 to 30 seconds per cupcake	HIGH	Fill cups half to two-thirds full of batter. Microwave until centers spring back when touched lightly, rotating 1 or 2 times. Let stand for 3 to 5 min.
Single Pie Crust	3 to 5 min.	HIGH	Thoroughly prick bottom and sides with fork. Microwave until dry and opaque, rotating pie plate 1 or 2 times. Cool.
Frozen Pie Crust, deep dish	4 to 5 min.	**5** to thaw, HIGH to cook	Remove packaging. Transfer crust to glass pie plate. Microwave for 45 to 60 seconds. Let stand for 2 to 3 minutes to finish thawing. Thoroughly prick bottom and sides with fork. Increase power to HIGH. Microwave for 3 to 4 minutes, or until dry and opaque, rotating pie place once. Cool.
Crumb Crust	1½ to 2 min.	HIGH	Microwave until set, rotating pie plate once. Cool.

◁

CIDER SPICE CAKE

Power Levels / HIGH, **5**
Approx. Cooking Time / 12 minutes
Yield / 1 ring cake

  3 to 4 tablespoons graham cracker crumbs
1¾ cups all-purpose flour
  2 teaspoons ground cinnamon
  1 teaspoon ground nutmeg
  1 teaspoon ground cloves
  ¾ teaspoon salt
  ¾ teaspoon baking soda
  ½ cup butter or margarine
  1 cup granulated sugar
  2 eggs
1¼ cups apple cider
  Powdered sugar

1 Grease 10 or 12-cup fluted ring dish. Sprinkle with graham cracker crumbs. Tilt dish to coat sides and bottom. Shake out and discard excess crumbs. Set dish aside.

2 In medium mixing bowl, combine flour, cinnamon, nutmeg, cloves, salt and baking soda. Stir. Set aside.

3 Place butter in another medium mixing bowl. Microwave at HIGH for 15 to 30 seconds, or until butter softens. Add granulated sugar and eggs. Cream at high speed of electric mixer. Add half of flour mixture. Beat at medium speed until smooth, scraping bowl occasionally. Add half of apple cider. Beat at medium speed until blended, scraping bowl occasionally. Repeat with remaining flour mixture and cider.

4 Pour batter into prepared dish. Place on saucer in oven. Microwave at POWER LEVEL **5** for 8 minutes, rotating dish once.

5 Increase power to HIGH. Microwave for about 4 minutes longer, or until edges begin to pull away from sides and knife inserted in center comes out clean. Let stand for 10 minutes. Invert onto serving plate. Cool slightly. Sprinkle with powdered sugar.

GLAZED RUM CAKE

Power Levels / **5**, HIGH
Approx. Cooking Time / 14 minutes
Yield / 1 ring cake

  3 to 4 tablespoons graham cracker crumbs

  CAKE

  1 pkg. (18¼ or 18½ oz.) yellow cake mix
  1 pkg. (3½ oz.) instant vanilla pudding and pie filling mix
  4 eggs
  ½ cup dark rum
  ½ cup vegetable oil
  ½ cup water

  GLAZE

  2 tablespoons dark rum
1½ tablespoons granulated sugar
  1 tablespoon butter or margarine
1½ tablespoons butter or margarine
  ½ cup powdered sugar

1 Grease 10 or 12-cup fluted ring dish. Sprinkle with graham cracker crumbs. Tilt dish to coat sides and bottom. Shake out and discard excess crumbs. Set dish aside.

2 For cake, in medium mixing bowl, combine all ingredients. Beat at medium speed of electric mixer for 3 minutes, scraping bowl occasionally. Pour into prepared dish. Place on saucer in oven. Microwave at POWER LEVEL **5** for 8 minutes, rotating dish once.

3 Increase power to HIGH. Microwave for 3½ to 4½ minutes longer, or until edges begin to pull away from sides and knife inserted in center comes out clean. Let stand for 10 minutes. Loosen edges. Invert onto serving plate.

4 For glaze, in small mixing bowl, combine rum, granulated sugar and 1 tablespoon butter. Microwave at HIGH for about 1½ minutes, or until sugar dissolves. Set aside.

5 Place 1½ tablespoons butter in medium mixing bowl. Microwave at HIGH for 10 to 20 seconds, or until butter softens. Add powdered sugar. Cream at high speed of electric mixer. Add rum mixture. Beat at medium speed until blended. Drizzle over cake.

CHOCOLATE APPLE CAKE △

Power Levels / HIGH, **7**
Approx. Cooking Time / 14 minutes
Yield / One 9-inch square cake

½ **cup butter or margarine**
2 **squares (1 oz. each) unsweetened chocolate**
1 **cup packed brown sugar**
2 **eggs**
½ **cup applesauce**
1 **teaspoon vanilla**
1 **cup all-purpose flour**
½ **teaspoon baking powder**
¼ **teaspoon baking soda**
1 **cup chopped, peeled apple**
Powdered sugar

1 In medium mixing bowl, combine butter
and chocolate. Microwave at HIGH for 2 to
2½ minutes, or until mixture can be stirred
smooth, stirring once. Blend in brown sugar,
eggs, applesauce and vanilla. Stir in flour,
baking powder and baking soda. Fold
in apples.

2 Pour batter into ungreased 9-inch square
baking dish. Shield corners of dish with
aluminum foil (page 138). Place on saucer in
oven. Microwave at POWER LEVEL **7** for
6 minutes, rotating dish once.

3 Remove foil. Microwave at POWER LEVEL **7**
for 4½ to 5½ minutes longer, or until center
springs back when touched lightly. Let stand
for 5 to 10 minutes. Cool slightly. Sprinkle
with powdered sugar.

PINEAPPLE UPSIDE-DOWN CAKE △

Power Levels / HIGH, **5**
Approx. Cooking Time / 13 minutes
Yield / One 9-inch round cake

3 **tablespoons butter or margarine**
¼ **cup packed brown sugar**
1 **tablespoon half-and-half**
1 **can (8 oz.) sliced pineapple packed in juice**
4 **maraschino cherries**
1 **pkg. (9 oz.) yellow cake mix (single layer)**

1 Line bottom of 9-inch round baking dish
with wax paper. Place butter in dish. Microwave at HIGH for 45 to 60 seconds, or until
butter melts.

2 Blend in brown sugar and half-and-half.
Microwave at HIGH for 1 minute, stirring
once. Drain pineapple, reserving juice.
Arrange pineapple slices and cherries on
brown sugar mixture.

3 Add enough water to pineapple juice to make
amount of liquid called for in cake mix
package directions. Prepare cake batter
according to package directions, using diluted
pineapple juice for liquid. Pour batter over
fruit in dish. Place on saucer in oven.
Microwave at POWER LEVEL **5** for 6
minutes, rotating dish once.

4 Increase power to HIGH. Microwave for 3 to 5
minutes longer, or until center springs back
when touched lightly. Let stand for 3 to 5
minutes. Invert onto serving plate.

VANILLA CAKE △

Power Levels / HIGH, **5**
Approx. Cooking Time / 27 minutes
Yield / One 2-layer cake

⅔ **cup butter or margarine**
1⅓ **cups sugar**
1 **cup milk**
3 **eggs**
2 **teaspoons vanilla**
2 **cups all-purpose flour**
2½ **teaspoons baking powder**
½ **teaspoon salt**
1 **recipe Chocolate Frosting, page 139**

1 Line bottoms of two 9-inch round baking
  dishes with wax paper. Set aside.

2 Place butter in medium mixing bowl.
  Microwave at HIGH for 15 to 30 seconds, or
  until butter softens. Add sugar. Cream at
  high speed of electric mixer. Add milk, eggs
  and vanilla. Add flour, baking powder and
  salt. Beat at low speed until dry ingredients
  are moistened, scraping bowl constantly.
  Beat at medium speed for 2 minutes, scraping
  bowl occasionally.

3 Pour batter into prepared dishes. Place 1 dish
  on saucer in oven. Microwave at POWER
  LEVEL **5** for 6 minutes, rotating dish once.
  Increase power to HIGH. Microwave for 3 to 5
  minutes longer, or until center springs back
  when touched lightly. Let stand for 5 to 10
  minutes. Invert onto wire rack. Cool. Repeat
  with remaining cake layer. Prepare frosting as
  directed. Spread on cooled cake.

GERMAN CHOCOLATE SNACK CAKE △

Power Levels / HIGH, **5**
Approx. Cooking Time / 13 minutes
Yield / One 9-inch round cake

3 **tablespoons butter or margarine**
¼ **cup packed brown sugar**
1 **tablespoon half-and-half**
⅔ **cup pecan halves or chopped pecans**
½ **cup flaked coconut**
1 **pkg. (9 oz.) chocolate cake mix (single layer)**

1 Line bottom of 9-inch round baking dish
  with wax paper. Place butter in dish. Microwave at HIGH for 45 to 60 seconds, or until
  butter melts.

2 Blend in brown sugar and half-and-half.
  Microwave at HIGH for 1 minute, stirring
  once. Sprinkle with pecans and coconut.

3 Prepare cake batter according to package
  directions. Pour over mixture in baking dish.
  Place on saucer in oven. Microwave at POWER
  LEVEL **5** for 6 minutes, rotating dish once.

4 Increase power to HIGH. Microwave for 3 to 5
  minutes longer, or until center springs back
  when touched lightly. Let stand for 5 to 10
  minutes. Invert onto serving plate.

CHOCOLATE POUND CAKE

Power Levels / **5**, HIGH
Approx. Cooking Time / 19 minutes
Yield / 1 tube cake

  2 tablespoons sugar
  2 squares (1 oz. each) semisweet chocolate
  1 cup butter or margarine
  1 cup sugar
  4 eggs
1½ cups all-purpose flour
  ½ teaspoon baking powder
  ½ teaspoon salt

1 Lightly grease 9-inch tube dish. Sprinkle with 2 tablespoons sugar. Tilt dish to coat bottom and sides. Shake out and discard excess sugar. Set dish aside.

2 Place chocolate in small bowl. Microwave at POWER LEVEL **5** for 5 to 6 minutes, or until chocolate can be stirred smooth, stirring 1 or 2 times. Set aside.

3 Place butter in large mixing bowl. Microwave at HIGH for 15 to 30 seconds, or until butter softens. Add 1 cup sugar. Cream at high speed of electric mixer. Add melted chocolate and eggs. Beat at medium speed until blended, scraping bowl frequently. Add remaining ingredients. Beat at medium speed for about 4 minutes, scraping bowl frequently.

4 Spoon batter into prepared dish. Place on saucer in oven. Microwave at POWER LEVEL **5** for 9 minutes, rotating dish 2 times.

5 Increase power to HIGH. Microwave for 3 to 4 minutes longer, or until top is almost dry and edges begin to pull away from sides. Let stand for 5 minutes. Loosen edges. Invert onto serving plate. Cover loosely with plastic wrap. Cool.

◁

CARROT CAKE

Power Levels / **7**, HIGH, **5**
Approx. Cooking Time / 17 minutes
Yield / One 9-inch square cake

1¼ cups all-purpose flour
  1 cup packed brown sugar
  1 teaspoon baking powder
  1 teaspoon baking soda
  1 teaspoon ground cinnamon
  ½ teaspoon ground allspice
  ½ teaspoon salt
  1 cup shredded carrot
  1 can (8 oz.) crushed pineapple, undrained
  ½ cup vegetable oil
  2 eggs
  1 teaspoon vanilla
  1 recipe Cream Cheese Frosting, opposite

1 In medium mixing bowl, mix flour, brown sugar, baking powder, baking soda, cinnamon, allspice and salt. Add remaining ingredients except frosting. Beat at medium speed of electric mixer for about 2 minutes, or until blended, scraping bowl frequently.

2 Pour into ungreased 9-inch square baking dish. Shield corners of dish with aluminum foil (below). Place on saucer in oven. Microwave at POWER LEVEL **7** for 6 minutes, rotating dish once.

3 Remove foil. Microwave at POWER LEVEL **7** for 8 to 10 minutes longer, or until center springs back when touched lightly and no uncooked batter remains on bottom of dish, rotating dish every 3 minutes. Cool. Prepare frosting as directed. Spread on cooled cake.

HOW TO SHIELD SQUARE BAKING DISH

SHIELD 9-inch square baking dish by molding a strip of aluminum foil over each corner.

CREAM CHEESE FROSTING

Power Levels / HIGH, **5**
Approx. Cooking Time / 1 minute
Yield / Frosts one 9-inch square cake

 3 tablespoons butter or margarine
 1 pkg. (3 oz.) cream cheese
 ⅛ teaspoon ground cinnamon
 1 to 1¼ cups powdered sugar

1 Place butter in small bowl. Microwave at
   HIGH for 10 to 20 seconds, or until butter
   softens. Set aside.

2 Place cream cheese in medium mixing bowl.
   Microwave at POWER LEVEL **5** for 30 to 60
   seconds, or until cream cheese softens. Add
   softened butter and cinnamon. Cream at
   medium speed of electric mixer. Beat in
   enough powdered sugar to make desired
   consistency. Spread on cooled cake.

CHOCOLATE FROSTING

Power Levels / **5**, HIGH
Approx. Cooking Time / 5 minutes
Yield / Fills and frosts two 9-inch layers

 2 squares (1 oz. each) unsweetened chocolate
 3 teaspoons butter or margarine
 2 tablespoons shortening
 3½ cups powdered sugar
 5 tablespoons half-and-half
 ½ teaspoon vanilla
 ⅛ teaspoon salt
 2 to 3 teaspoons half-and-half (optional)

1 Place chocolate in medium mixing bowl.
   Microwave at POWER LEVEL **5** for 4 to 5
   minutes, or until chocolate can be stirred
   smooth, stirring 1 or 2 times. Cool slightly.

2 Place butter in small bowl. Microwave at
   HIGH for 15 to 30 seconds, or until butter
   softens. Add to chocolate. Add shortening.
   Cream at high speed of electric mixer. Add
   remaining ingredients. Beat at high speed
   until smooth. If necessary, add additional
   half-and-half, 1 teaspoon at a time, to make
   desired consistency.

TIP ▪ To make cake easier to frost, place cooled
cake layers in freezer for about 30 minutes
before frosting.

CHOCOLATE CHEESE PIE ▽

Power Levels / HIGH, **5**
Approx. Cooking Time / 24 minutes
Yield / One 9-inch pie

 1 recipe Graham Cracker Crust, page 141
 1 pkg. (8 oz.) cream cheese
 ½ cup sugar
 2 eggs
 1 teaspoon vanilla
 1 square (1 oz.) semisweet chocolate
 ½ cup dairy sour cream
 1 can (21 oz.) prepared cherry pie filling (optional)

1 Prepare and microwave crust as directed.
   Set aside.

2 Place cream cheese in medium mixing bowl.
   Microwave at POWER LEVEL **5** for 1½ to 2
   minutes, or until cream cheese softens. Add
   sugar, eggs and vanilla. Beat at low speed of
   electric mixer until blended. Set aside.

3 Place chocolate in small bowl. Microwave at
   POWER LEVEL **5** for 3½ to 4½ minutes, or
   until chocolate can be stirred smooth, stirring
   1 or 2 times. Add to cream cheese mixture. Add
   sour cream. Beat at low speed until smooth.

4 Pour into prepared crust. Place on saucer in
   oven. Microwave at POWER LEVEL **5** for 12
   to 15 minutes, or until center is slightly set,
   rotating pie plate every 3 minutes. Let stand
   for 10 minutes. Chill for 6 hours, or until set.
   Top with cherry pie filling.

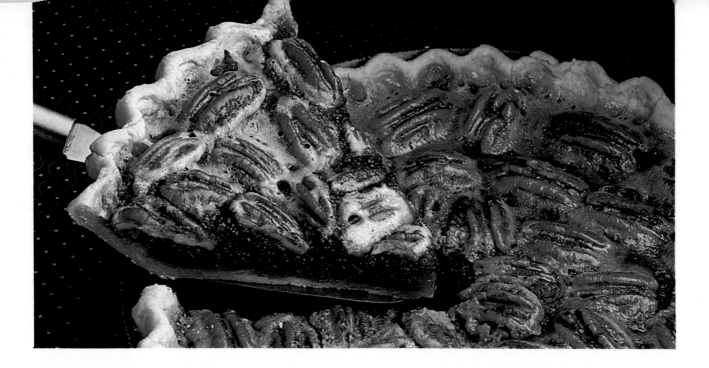

PECAN PIE △

Power Levels / HIGH, **5**
Approx. Cooking Time / 25 minutes
Yield / One 9-inch pie

 1 recipe Single Pie Crust, opposite
 2 tablespoons butter or margarine
 1 cup dark corn syrup
 3 eggs
⅓ cup packed dark brown sugar
 1 tablespoon all-purpose flour
 1 teaspoon vanilla
¾ cup pecan halves or chopped pecans

1 Prepare and microwave crust as directed (follow directions in **TIP**). Set aside.

2 Place butter in medium mixing bowl. Microwave at HIGH for 45 to 60 seconds, or until butter melts. Add remaining ingredients except pecans. Beat at medium speed of electric mixer for 1 to 2 minutes, or until smooth, scraping bowl occasionally. Stir in pecans.

3 Pour into prepared crust. Place on saucer in oven. Microwave at POWER LEVEL **5** for 15 to 17 minutes, or until set, rotating pie plate every 5 minutes. Cool completely.

WALNUT PIE

Follow recipe above, substituting walnut halves or chopped walnuts for pecans.

COCONUT LEMON MERINGUE PIE

Power Level / HIGH
Approx. Cooking Time / 20 minutes
Yield / One 9-inch pie

 1 recipe Single Pie Crust, opposite
2¼ cups water
 1 pkg. (3 oz.) lemon pudding and pie filling mix
½ cup sugar
 2 eggs, separated
⅓ cup flaked coconut
¼ cup sugar

1 Prepare and microwave crust as directed (follow directions in **TIP**). Set aside.

2 In medium mixing bowl, blend water, pudding mix, ½ cup sugar and 2 egg yolks. Microwave at HIGH for 5½ to 6 minutes, or until mixture thickens, stirring 2 or 3 times. Cool for 5 minutes. Pour into prepared crust. Cool for 10 minutes longer.

3 Meanwhile, sprinkle coconut on plate. Microwave at HIGH for 3 to 5 minutes, or until coconut lightly browns, stirring after every minute.

4 Place egg whites in medium mixing bowl. Beat at high speed of electric mixer until foamy. Gradually add ¼ cup sugar while continuing to beat until stiff peaks form. Spread on pie, gently pushing to edge to seal. Sprinkle with coconut. Microwave at HIGH for 2 to 2½ minutes, or until meringue is set. Chill for 4 hours, or until set.

GRASSHOPPER PIE ▷

Power Levels / HIGH, **7**
Approx. Cooking Time / 7 minutes
Yield / One 9-inch pie

1 recipe Chocolate Crumb Crust, below
3 cups miniature marshmallows
½ cup half-and-half or milk
3 tablespoons white crème de cacao
3 tablespoons green crème de menthe
1 cup whipping cream

1 Prepare and microwave crust as directed.
   Set aside.

2 In medium mixing bowl, combine marshmallows and half-and-half. Microwave at
   POWER LEVEL **7** for 3½ to 4½ minutes, or
   until mixture can be stirred smooth. Stir in
   crème de cacao and crème de menthe.
   Refrigerate for about 30 minutes, or until
   mixture slightly thickens.

3 Pour whipping cream into chilled medium
   mixing bowl. Beat at high speed of electric
   mixer until soft peaks form. Fold in marshmallow mixture. Spread in prepared crust.
   Chill for 4 hours, or until set.

GRAHAM CRACKER CRUST

Power Level / HIGH
Approx. Cooking Time / 3 minutes
Yield / One 9-inch crust

¼ cup butter or margarine
1¼ cups fine graham cracker crumbs
¼ cup sugar

1 Place butter in 9-inch pie plate. Microwave at
   HIGH for 45 seconds to 1¼ minutes, or until
   butter melts. Stir in graham cracker crumbs
   and sugar.

2 Press mixture evenly on bottom and side of
   pie plate. Microwave at HIGH for 1½ to 2
   minutes, or until set, rotating pie plate
   once. Cool.

CHOCOLATE CRUMB CRUST

Follow recipe above, substituting crushed
chocolate wafers for graham cracker crumbs.
Omit sugar.

SINGLE PIE CRUST

Power Level / HIGH
Approx. Cooking Time / 6 minutes
Yield / One 9-inch crust

1¼ cups all-purpose flour
¼ teaspoon salt
⅓ cup plus 1 tablespoon shortening
2 to 4 tablespoons ice water
1½ teaspoons butter or margarine
1½ teaspoons vanilla

1 In medium mixing bowl, mix flour and salt.
   Cut in shortening to form coarse crumbs.
   Sprinkle in water, 1 tablespoon at a time,
   stirring with fork until particles are moistened
   and cling together. Form dough into a ball.
   Roll out on lightly-floured board to a circle at
   least 2 inches larger than inverted 9-inch pie
   plate. Ease into plate. Trim and flute edge.
   Thoroughly prick bottom and side with fork.

2 Place butter in small bowl. Microwave at
   HIGH for 45 to 60 seconds, or until butter
   melts. Blend in vanilla. Brush evenly on
   bottom and side of crust. Microwave at HIGH
   for 4 to 5 minutes, or until crust is dry and
   opaque, rotating pie plate once. Cool.

**TIP ▪ If filling crust with liquid mixture, prepare
and microwave as directed. Then in small bowl,
mix 1 egg yolk and 2 teaspoons milk. Brush on
bottom and side of hot crust. Microwave at HIGH
for 30 to 60 seconds, or until yolk mixture is set.
This prevents crust from getting soggy.**

◁

ALMOND BUTTER CRUNCH

Power Level / HIGH
Approx. Cooking Time / 15 minutes
Yield / About 1 lb.

 2 tablespoons butter or margarine
½ cup slivered almonds
½ cup butter or margarine, cut into chunks
1½ cups sugar
 3 tablespoons water
 1 tablespoon light corn syrup
 2 bars (about 1½ oz. each) milk chocolate, broken into small pieces

1 Line baking sheet with aluminum foil. Butter foil. Set aside.

2 Place 2 tablespoons butter in shallow bowl. Microwave at HIGH for 45 to 60 seconds, or until butter melts.

3 Stir in almonds. Microwave at HIGH for 4 to 5 minutes, or until almonds lightly brown, stirring after every minute. Drain on paper towels. Sprinkle almonds on prepared baking sheet in 12 x 8-inch area. Set aside.

4 In 2-quart measure or medium mixing bowl, combine remaining ingredients except chocolate. Microwave at HIGH for 2 to 3 minutes, or until sugar dissolves and mixture can be stirred smooth, stirring once. Place microwave candy thermometer in mixture. Microwave at HIGH for 5½ to 6½ minutes longer, or until temperature registers 300°F. Continue according to photo directions below.

HOW TO ASSEMBLE ALMOND BUTTER CRUNCH

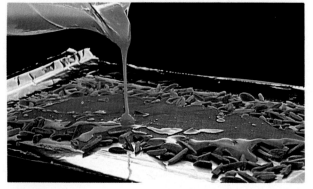

POUR mixture over almonds. Let stand for 1 minute. Arrange chocolate on top of candy.

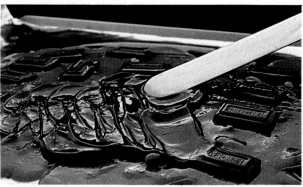

LET STAND for 2 to 3 minutes, or until chocolate melts. Spread chocolate over candy. Chill to set. Break into pieces.

CARAMEL NUT BARS △

Power Levels / **5**, HIGH
Approx. Cooking Time / 8 minutes
Yield / 2 dozen bars

⅓ **cup butter or margarine, cut into chunks**
¾ **cup all-purpose flour**
¾ **cup quick-cooking rolled oats**
¼ **cup packed brown sugar**
¼ **teaspoon salt**
½ **cup caramel topping**
½ **cup powdered sugar**
¼ **teaspoon vanilla**
½ **cup chopped nuts**

1 In medium mixing bowl, combine butter,
   flour, oats, brown sugar and salt. Beat at low
   speed of electric mixer until mixture forms
   coarse crumbs. Pat mixture in bottom of 9-inch
   square baking dish. Place on saucer in oven.
   Microwave at POWER LEVEL **5** for 5 to 6
   minutes, or until set, rotating dish once.
   Set aside.

2 In 4-cup measure or small mixing bowl, mix
   caramel topping, powdered sugar and vanilla.
   Microwave at HIGH for about 2 minutes, or
   until mixture bubbles, stirring 2 times. Stir in
   nuts. Spread evenly over crust. Chill to set.
   Cut into 24 bars.

CHOCOLATE RAISIN CLUSTERS △

Power Level / HIGH
Approx. Cooking Time / 4 minutes
Yield / About 2 dozen

8 **squares (1 oz. each) semisweet chocolate**
⅔ **cup sweetened condensed milk**
1½ **cups raisins**

1 Line baking sheet with wax paper. Set aside.
   Place chocolate in small mixing bowl. Microwave at HIGH for 3 to 4 minutes, or until
   chocolate can be stirred smooth, stirring
   1 or 2 times.

2 Blend in condensed milk. Stir in raisins. Drop
   by heaping teaspoonfuls onto prepared
   baking sheet. Chill to set.

CHOCOLATE PEANUT CLUSTERS

Follow recipe above, substituting salted peanuts
for raisins.

CHOCOLATE RAISIN NUT CLUSTERS

Follow recipe above, reducing raisins to ¾ cup.
Stir in ¾ cup chopped nuts with raisins.

CHOCOLATE HAYSTACKS

Follow recipe above, substituting chow mein
noodles for raisins.

◁
FUDGE

Power Levels / HIGH, **7**
Approx. Cooking Time / 7 minutes
Yield / About 2 lbs.

1⅓ **cups sugar**
  1 **can (5⅓ oz.) evaporated milk**
  1 **tablespoon butter or margarine**
  1 **pkg. (12 oz.) semisweet chocolate chips**
½ **cup marshmallow creme**
½ **cup chopped nuts (optional)**
1½ **teaspoons vanilla**

1 Butter 9-inch square baking dish. Set aside.

2 In 2-quart casserole or medium mixing bowl, combine sugar, evaporated milk and butter. Microwave at HIGH for 3 to 4 minutes, or until mixture boils, stirring after every minute.

3 Reduce to POWER LEVEL **7**. Microwave for 3 to 3½ minutes longer, or until sugar dissolves, stirring 1 or 2 times to prevent boil over. Add remaining ingredients. Stir until chocolate melts and mixture is blended. Pour into prepared dish. Chill to set.

◁
NUTTY CHOCOLATE BARS

Power Levels / HIGH, **7**
Approx. Cooking Time / 10 minutes
Yield / 2 dozen bars

¼ **cup butter or margarine**
¾ **cup graham cracker crumbs**
  1 **can (14 oz.) sweetened condensed milk**
½ **cup semisweet chocolate chips**
½ **cup flaked coconut**
  1 **cup chopped nuts**

1 Place butter in 9-inch square baking dish. Microwave at HIGH for 45 seconds to 1¼ minutes, or until butter melts. Stir in graham cracker crumbs. Press mixture evenly in bottom of dish.

2 Pour condensed milk evenly over crust. Sprinkle with chocolate chips and coconut. Top with half the nuts. Lightly press down. Place on saucer in oven. Microwave at POWER LEVEL **7** for 8 to 9 minutes, or until mixture bubbles, rotating dish every 2 minutes. Sprinkle with remaining nuts. Cool. Cut into 24 bars.

QUICK RICE PUDDING ▷

Power Level / HIGH
Approx. Cooking Time / 8 minutes
Yield / 4 to 6 servings

  1 pkg. (3⅛ oz.) vanilla pudding and pie filling mix
2½ cups milk
 ½ cup uncooked instant rice
 ¼ cup raisins
 ¼ teaspoon ground nutmeg
   Ground nutmeg (optional)

1 Place pudding mix in 1½-quart casserole.
   Gradually blend in milk. Stir in rice, raisins
   and ¼ teaspoon nutmeg. Microwave at HIGH
   for about 8 minutes, or until mixture thickens,
   stirring 2 or 3 times.

2 Refrigerate for about 30 minutes. Stir. Sprinkle
   with nutmeg. Chill.

CHOCOLATE RICE PUDDING

Follow recipe above, substituting chocolate pudding mix for vanilla pudding mix. Omit nutmeg.

INDIVIDUAL BAKED CUSTARDS

Power Levels / HIGH, **5**
Approx. Cooking Time / 19 minutes
Yield / 6 servings

 4 eggs
⅓ cup sugar
½ teaspoon vanilla
¼ teaspoon salt
 2 cups milk
   Ground nutmeg (optional)

1 In medium mixing bowl, blend eggs, sugar,
   vanilla and salt. Set aside.

2 Pour milk into 4-cup measure or small mixing
   bowl. Microwave at HIGH for about 4
   minutes, or until scalded. Blend into egg
   mixture. Divide mixture evenly among six
   6-ounce custard cups. Sprinkle with nutmeg.

3 Arrange cups in a circle in oven. Microwave at
   POWER LEVEL **5** for 13 to 15 minutes, or
   until custards are soft set, rearranging 2 or 3
   times and removing from oven as they finish
   cooking. Let stand for 5 minutes. Serve warm
   or chilled.

RAISIN BREAD PUDDING

Power Levels / HIGH, **5**
Approx. Cooking Time / 21 minutes
Yield / 6 to 8 servings

¼ cup sugar
⅛ teaspoon ground cinnamon
 3 cups cubed raisin bread, ¾-inch cubes
   (4 to 5 slices)
 5 eggs
½ cup sugar
 1 teaspoon vanilla
 2 cups milk
¼ cup butter or margarine
   Whipped cream (optional)

1 In 1½-quart casserole, combine ¼ cup sugar
   and the cinnamon. Add bread cubes. Toss to
   coat. Set aside. In medium mixing bowl, blend
   eggs, ½ cup sugar and the vanilla. Set aside.

2 In 4-cup measure or small mixing bowl,
   combine milk and butter. Microwave at HIGH
   for about 4 minutes, or until milk is scalded.
   Blend into egg mixture.

3 Pour mixture over bread cubes. Cover dish
   with wax paper. Microwave at POWER LEVEL
   5 for 15 to 17 minutes, or until center is soft set,
   breaking up and pushing edges toward center
   with rubber spatula 2 times. Let stand for 10 to
   15 minutes. Garnish with whipped cream.

STRAWBERRY PEACH COBBLER △

Power Level / HIGH
Approx. Cooking Time / 23 minutes
Yield / 6 to 8 servings

1 pkg. (16 oz.) frozen peach slices
1 pkg. (10 oz.) frozen sweetened strawberries
2 tablespoons all-purpose flour
¼ teaspoon ground cinnamon
2 tablespoons butter or margarine
½ cup sliced almonds
2 tablespoons sugar
⅛ teaspoon ground cinnamon
2 tablespoons butter or margarine
1 cup buttermilk baking mix
¼ cup half-and-half
Half-and-half (optional)

1 Remove peaches and strawberries from packaging and place in medium mixing bowl. Microwave at HIGH for 4 to 6 minutes, or until fruit can be broken apart. Let stand for 5 to 10 minutes. Drain juices into 1½-quart casserole. Set fruit aside.

2 Blend flour and ¼ teaspoon cinnamon into fruit juices. Microwave at HIGH for 3 to 4 minutes, or until mixture thickens, stirring 1 or 2 times. Stir in reserved fruit. Set aside.

3 Place 2 tablespoons butter in shallow bowl. Microwave at HIGH for 45 to 60 seconds, or until butter melts. Stir in almonds. Microwave at HIGH for 4 to 5 minutes, or until almonds lightly brown. Stir in sugar and ⅛ teaspoon cinnamon. Set aside.

4 Place 2 tablespoons butter in small mixing bowl. Microwave at HIGH for 45 to 60 seconds, or until butter melts. Add baking mix and ¼ cup half-and-half. Mix well. Drop by heaping tablespoonfuls onto fruit mixture. Sprinkle with almond mixture. Microwave at HIGH for 5 to 6 minutes, or until dumplings spring back when touched lightly, rotating dish 2 times. Serve warm with half-and-half.

BAKED APPLES ▷

Power Level / HIGH
Approx. Cooking Time / 9 minutes
Yield / 4 servings

4 large baking apples (8 to 10 oz. each)
¼ cup packed brown sugar
2 tablespoons raisins or finely-chopped nuts
¼ teaspoon ground cinnamon
2 tablespoons butter or margarine, cut into 4
  chunks

1 Core apples. Peel skin from top 1 inch of
  each apple.

2 In small dish, combine brown sugar, raisins
  and cinnamon. Stuff each apple with an equal
  amount of raisin mixture. Dot top of each
  apple with 1 chunk of butter.

3 Arrange apples in 9-inch square baking dish.
  Cover dish with plastic wrap. Microwave at
  HIGH for 7 to 9 minutes, or until apples are
  tender, rotating dish once. Let stand for 5
  minutes. Just before serving, spoon juices
  from bottom of baking dish over apples.

APPLESAUCE

Power Level / HIGH
Approx. Cooking Time / 12 minutes
Yield / About 4 cups

3 lbs. baking apples, peeled, cored and sliced
½ to ¾ cup sugar
⅓ to ½ cup water
½ to 1 teaspoon ground cinnamon

1 In large mixing bowl, combine all ingredients.
  Cover bowl with wax paper. Microwave at
  HIGH for 10 to 12 minutes, or until apples are
  tender, stirring 2 times.

2 Mash or purée until sauce is desired
  consistency. Serve warm or chilled.

SPICED GRAPE JELLY ▽

Power Level / HIGH
Approx. Cooking Time / 19 minutes
Yield / About 4 cups

3½ cups sugar
  2 cups grape juice
  6 whole cloves
  6 whole allspice
  1 stick cinnamon
  1 pouch (3 oz.) liquid pectin (half of 6-oz. pkg.)

1 In 5-quart casserole, mix sugar and grape
   juice. Add cloves, allspice and cinnamon.
   Microwave at HIGH for 10 to 12 minutes, or
   until mixture boils, stirring 2 times during first
   4 minutes to dissolve sugar.

2 Stir in pectin. Microwave at HIGH for 4 to 6
   minutes, or until mixture comes to full rolling
   boil. Boil for 1 minute. Skim and discard foam
   and spices.

3 Ladle jam into clean, hot jars. Store covered
   in refrigerator or in sealed jars.

PEACH JAM ▽

Power Level / HIGH
Approx. Cooking Time / 36 minutes
Yield / 9 cups

  3 pkgs. (1 lb. each) frozen peach slices
7¼ cups sugar
  ¼ cup lemon juice
  1 pouch (3 oz.) liquid pectin (half of 6-oz. pkg.)

1 Remove peaches from packaging and place
   in 5-quart casserole. Microwave at HIGH for
   9 to 10 minutes, or until thawed, stirring every
   3 minutes to break apart. Let stand for
   5 to 10 minutes.

2 Drain peaches, discarding liquid. Stir in sugar
   and lemon juice. Microwave at HIGH for 23 to
   25 minutes, or until mixture comes to full
   rolling boil, stirring 3 or 4 times to dissolve
   sugar. Boil for 1 minute. Add pectin. Stir for
   5 minutes. Skim and discard foam.

3 Ladle jam into clean, hot jars. Store covered
   in refrigerator or in sealed jars.

STRAWBERRY RASPBERRY JAM △

Power Level / HIGH
Approx. Cooking Time / 39 minutes
Yield / About 7 cups

- 3 pkgs. (10 oz. each) frozen strawberries in heavy syrup
- 1 pkg. (10 oz.) frozen raspberries in heavy syrup
- 5 cups sugar
- 2 tablespoons lemon juice
- ⅛ teaspoon ground cinnamon
- 1 pouch (3 oz.) liquid pectin (half of 6-oz. pkg.)

1 Remove strawberries and raspberries from packaging and place in 5-quart casserole. Microwave at HIGH for 8 to 10 minutes, or until thawed, stirring 2 times to break apart. Let stand for 5 to 10 minutes.

2 Stir in sugar, lemon juice and cinnamon. Microwave at HIGH for 22 to 28 minutes, or until mixture comes to full rolling boil, stirring 3 or 4 times to dissolve sugar. Boil for 1 minute. Add pectin. Stir for 5 minutes. Skim and discard foam.

3 Ladle jam into clean, hot jars. Store covered in refrigerator or in sealed jars.

ORANGE PINEAPPLE JAM △

Power Level / HIGH
Approx. Cooking Time / 25 minutes
Yield / About 7 cups

- 1 can (20 oz.) crushed pineapple packed in juice, undrained
- 1 can (11 oz.) mandarin orange segments, drained and chopped
  Water
- 6 cups sugar
- ½ cup lemon juice
- 1 pouch (3 oz.) liquid pectin (half of 6-oz. pkg.)

1 In 4-cup glass measure, combine crushed pineapple and orange segments. Add enough water to make 3½ cups.

2 In 5-quart casserole, combine pineapple mixture, sugar and lemon juice. Microwave at HIGH for 22 to 24 minutes, or until mixture comes to full rolling boil, stirring occasionally during first 7 minutes to dissolve sugar. Boil for 1 minute. Add pectin. Stir for 5 minutes. Skim and discard foam.

3 Ladle jam into clean, hot jars. Store covered in refrigerator or in sealed jars.

PEACH LIQUEUR △

Power Levels / **7**, **1**
Approx. Cooking Time / 40 minutes
Yield / About 2 cups

1½ lbs. frozen sliced peaches (about 6 cups)
2 cups bourbon
1½ cups sugar
4 strips lemon peel
2 sticks cinnamon
3 whole cloves

1 Remove peaches from packaging and place in medium mixing bowl. Add remaining ingredients. Microwave at POWER LEVEL **7** for 10 minutes, stirring 2 times to dissolve sugar.

2 Reduce to POWER LEVEL **1**. Microwave for 30 minutes longer, stirring 2 times.

3 Cover bowl with plastic wrap. Leave in cool place for at least 3 days before serving. Strain. Store liqueur covered in cool, dark place.

CHERRY ALMOND LIQUEUR △

Power Levels / **7**, **1**
Approx. Cooking Time / 40 minutes
Yield / About 2 cups

1 pkg. (1 lb.) frozen pitted dark sweet cherries
2 cups vodka
1 cup sugar
½ teaspoon almond extract

1 In medium mixing bowl, combine all ingredients. Microwave at POWER LEVEL **7** for 10 minutes, stirring 2 times to dissolve sugar.

2 Reduce to POWER LEVEL **1**. Microwave for 30 minutes longer, stirring 2 times.

3 Cover bowl with plastic wrap. Leave in cool place for at least 3 days before serving. Strain. Store liqueur covered in cool, dark place.

APRICOT BRANDY △

Power Levels / **7**, **1**
Approx. Cooking Time / 39 minutes
Yield / About 2 cups

2 pkgs. (6 oz. each) dried apricots
2 cups brandy
1¾ cups sugar

1 In medium mixing bowl, mix all ingredients.
   Microwave at POWER LEVEL **7** for 8 to 9
   minutes, stirring 2 times to dissolve sugar.

2 Reduce to POWER LEVEL **1**. Microwave for
   30 minutes longer, stirring 2 times.

3 Cover bowl with plastic wrap. Leave in cool
   place for at least 3 days before serving. Strain.
   Store brandy covered in cool, dark place.

TIP ▪ Serve strained fruit from liqueurs and
brandy over ice cream or cake.

HERB GARLIC VINEGAR △

Power Level / HIGH
Approx. Cooking Time / 1 minute
Yield / 1½ cups

2 cloves garlic
1½ cups white or cider vinegar
½ teaspoon dried tarragon or rosemary leaves

1 Thread garlic cloves onto a 6-inch wooden
   skewer. Place in 16-oz. bottle or jar.* Add
   vinegar and tarragon. Microwave at HIGH for
   about 1 minute, or until bottle is just warm.

2 Cover with lid. Leave in cool, dark place for
   about 2 weeks before serving. Strain portion
   to be used, if desired. Store vinegar covered in
   refrigerator. Use within 2 months.

*Be sure bottle or jar is not flawed, chipped or
cracked.

DOUGH ART

2 cups all-purpose flour
1 cup salt
1 cup water

1 In medium mixing bowl, mix flour and salt. Gradually add water, stirring until mixture forms a ball. Knead on floured surface for 7 to 10 minutes, or until dough is smooth. Store in plastic food storage bag until ready for use (up to 2 days).

2 If preparing ornaments, rope ornaments or miniatures, spray baking sheet with vegetable cooking spray. Shape dough as desired according to opposite page. Microwave at POWER LEVEL **5** as directed, or until dough is firm and almost dry. Transfer shapes to wire rack. Allow to dry for at least 24 hours before decorating. Use water or enamel paints, or felt-tip markers to color dried shapes.

TIPS

• Attach two pieces of dough by moistening with water or pinching. Keep thickness of shapes less than ½ inch for best results.

• Add texture to painted shapes by sprinkling wet paint with fine white sand or granulated sugar. Apply another coat of paint, if desired.

• Glue magnets to miniatures after decorating, or use a drinking straw to make holes in ornaments before microwaving so they can be hung.

• Spray finished shapes with acrylic spray or shellac, or brush with varnish to keep dough and paint from cracking. Sprinkle wet coating with glitter, if desired.

HOW TO SHAPE DOUGH

ORNAMENTS. On floured surface, roll small amount of dough to ¼-inch thickness. Cut into shapes with 2½ to 3-inch diameter cookie cutters. Arrange 4 or 5 items on prepared baking sheet. Microwave for 4 to 6 minutes, rotating baking sheet every 2 minutes.

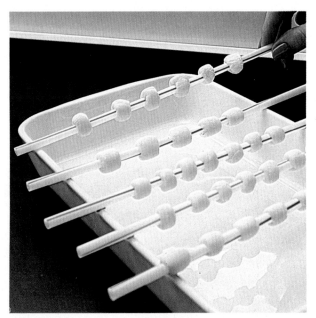

BEADS. Shape 8 small pieces of dough into 8 balls (beads) around a plastic drinking straw. Balance straw between edges of baking dish. Microwave for about 1 minute. Remove beads from straw before cooling.

ROPE ORNAMENTS. Use floured fingers to roll dough into rope-like shapes, 12 to 14 inches long and ¼ inch thick. Shape into letters or numbers. Arrange 4 items on prepared baking sheet. Microwave for 2 to 3 minutes, rotating baking sheet once.

MINIATURES. On floured surface, roll small amount of dough to ¼ to ½-inch thickness. Cut into shapes up to 1½ inches in diameter using cookie cutters, caps from spice bottles or a thin knife blade. Arrange 2 items on prepared baking sheet. Microwave for 2 to 3 minutes, rotating baking sheet once.

DRYING FLOWERS

Flowers
Silica gel or uncolored kitty litter*
Floral wire
Floral tape

Dry flowers according to photo directions on opposite page.

***Sift kitty litter, discarding larger pieces.**

TIPS

• Choose brightly-colored flowers that are partially open. White and pastel flowers may turn brown.

• Spray dried flowers with hair spray or acrylic spray coating for protection. Let spray dry completely.

FLOWER DRYING GUIDE

FLOWER	NUMBER OF FLOWERS IN OVEN	POWER LEVEL	TOTAL TIME
Carnation	2	9	3 to 3½ min.
Daisy	2	9	1 to 2 min.
Daisy Mums (Pom Poms)	2	9	3 to 4 min.
Rose	1	9	2½ to 3 min.

HOW TO DRY FLOWERS

TRIM stems ½ to ¾ inch from base of flowers. Spread silica gel, 1 to 2 inches deep, in small glass or paper bowl, or 2-cup measure. Prepare 1 container for each flower.

ARRANGE 1 flower, blossom-side up, in each bowl of silica gel. Sprinkle additional silica gel between petals, covering flower(s) completely.

PLACE 1 or 2 flowers in oven as directed in chart. Place 2-cup measure filled with water in oven. Microwave as directed. Remove from oven and allow to finish drying for at least 12 hours.

REMOVE flowers carefully, shaking gently to remove silica gel. Use small paintbrush to remove any remaining gel. Attach floral wire to stems with floral tape.

Index

A

Acorn Squash, Chart, 112
  Softening, 21
Almond Butter Crunch, 142
Appetizer Pâté, 24
Appetizers,
  Cheese Ball, 26
  Cheese 'n Bacon Sticks, 28
  Cocktail Reubens, 25
  Crab Meat Supreme, 29
  Curried Almonds, 26
  Garlic Shrimp, 26
  Ham Roll-Ups, 29
  Hot Mexicali Party Dip, 29
  Italian Vegetables, 28
  Mexicali Party Dip, 29
  Stuffed Mushrooms, 24
  Tangy Shrimp, 26
  Texas-Style Nachos, 29
Applesauce, 147
Apple-Stuffed Pork Chops, 65
Apricot Brandy, 153
Apricot Tea, 43
Arranging, 12, 13, 17
Asparagus, 112

B

Bacon, Chart, 63
Bacon and Egg Ring, 105
Baked Apples, 147
Baked Herb Tomatoes, 118
Banana Nut Coffee Cake, 129
Barbecued Beef Short Ribs, 50
Barley Mushroom Casserole, 125
Beans, Chart, 112
  Green Beans Amandine, 118
  Sausage and Bean Casserole, 69
  Savory Bean Bake, 115
Beef, Charts, 46, 47
  see also Ground Beef
  Barbecued Beef Short Ribs, 50
  Braised Beef Brisket, 49
  Corned Beef and Cabbage, 48
  Easy Stuffed Beef Rolls, 50
  Italian Marinated Roast, 48
  Marinated Sirloin Tip Roast, 48
  Old-Fashioned Pot Roast, 49
  Orange Braised Roast, 48
  Oriental Beef and Broccoli, 53
  Stuffed Beef Rolls, 50
  Vegetable Beef Soup, 34
Beef Bourguignon, 51
Beef Ragout, 51
Beef Stew, 54
Beef Stroganoff, 52
Beets, Chart, 112
Beverages, Chart, 41
  Apricot Tea, 43
  Cranberry Warmer, 41
  Creamy Cocoa, 40
  Hot Buttered Rum, 42
  Hot Butterscotch, 42
  Mocha Cocoa, 40
  Mulled Cider, 41
  Orange Warm-Up, 43
  Tips for Microwaving, 41
Blueberry Nut Bread, 128
Braised Beef Brisket, 49
Brandied Cherry Sauce, 109

Brandy,
  Apricot Brandy, 153
Breads,
  Blueberry Nut Bread, 128
  Breakfast Spice Muffins, 131
  Chili Cheese Cornbread, 130
  Muffins, 134
  Nut Bread, 128
  Pumpkin Muffins, 130
  Raisin Nut Bread, 128
Breakfast Spice Muffins, 131
Broccoli, Chart, 112
  Cream of Broccoli Soup, 32
  Oriental Beef and Broccoli, 53
Browning, 14, 15
Brown Sugar,
  Softening, 20
Brunswick Stew, 87
Brussels Sprouts, 112
Butter,
  Melting, 20

C

Cabbage, Chart, 112
  Corned Beef and Cabbage, 48
  Oriental Pork and Cabbage, 66
  Sausage with Sweet-and-Sour
    Cabbage, 73
  Savory Cabbage Rolls, 55
Cakes, Chart, 134
  Carrot Cake, 138
  Chocolate Apple Cake, 136
  Chocolate Pound Cake, 138
  Cider Spice Cake, 135
  German Chocolate Snack Cake, 137
  Glazed Rum Cake, 135
  Pineapple Upside-Down Cake, 136
  Vanilla Cake, 137
Candies,
  Almond Butter Crunch, 142
  Chocolate Haystacks, 143
  Chocolate Peanut Clusters, 143
  Chocolate Raisin Clusters, 143
  Chocolate Raisin Nut Clusters, 143
  Fudge, 144
Caramel Nut Bars, 143
Caramel Sauce, 108
Carrot Cake, 138
Carrots, Chart, 112
  Glazed Carrot Coins, 119
Cauliflower, 112
Cereals, Chart, 124
  see also Farina, Grits, Oats
Cheese and Bacon Hot Dogs, 37
Cheese and Mushroom Ham Loaf, 70
Cheese Ball, 26
Cheese 'n Bacon Sticks, 28
Cheese Sauce, 108
Cheesy Chicken with Chives, 88
Cherry Almond Liqueur, 152
Cherry Breakfast Ring, 128
Chicken, Charts, 82, 83
  Brunswick Stew, 87
  Cheesy Chicken with Chives, 88
  Easy Paella, 87
  Herbed Lemon Chicken, 88
  Quick Chicken and Vegetables, 89
  Rosemary-Simmered Chicken, 84
  Western Chicken, 86
Chicken À La King, 91
Chicken Amandine, 91
Chicken Gumbo, 36

Chicken Parmesan, 89
Chicken Tetrazzini, 90
Chicken with Creamy Mushroom
  Sauce, 86
Chili, 54
Chili Cheese Cornbread, 130
Chocolate,
  Melting, 20
Chocolate Apple Cake, 136
Chocolate Cheese Pie, 139
Chocolate Crumb Crust, 141
Chocolate Frosting, 139
Chocolate Haystacks, 143
Chocolate Peanut Clusters, 143
Chocolate Pound Cake, 138
Chocolate Raisin Clusters, 143
Chocolate Raisin Nut Clusters, 143
Chocolate Rice Pudding, 145
Cider Spice Cake, 135
Cinnamon Apricot Oatmeal, 124
Cinnamon Raisin Oatmeal, 124
Citrus Fruits,
  Juicing, 20
Citrus Noodles, 122
Classic Lamb Curry, 79
Cocktail Reubens, 25
Coconut Lemon Meringue Pie, 140
Coffee Cakes,
  Banana Nut Coffee Cake, 129
  Cherry Breakfast Ring, 128
  Cranberry Orange Coffee Ring, 129
  Poppy Seed Coffee Cake, 131
Containers for Microwaving, 7, 8
Converting Conventional Recipes, 18
Cooking Principles, 10, 11
Coquille Newfoundland, 97
Corn, Chart, 113
  Swiss Scalloped Corn, 118
Corned Beef and Cabbage, 48
Cornish Hens, Charts, 82, 83
Cornish Hens with Apple Sausage
  Stuffing, 85
Country Ham Casserole, 68
Coverings, 9
Crab,
  Easy Crab À La King, 97
Crab Meat Supreme, 29
Cranberry Orange Coffee Ring, 129
Cranberry Sauce, 115
Cranberry Warmer, 41
Cream Cheese,
  Softening, 20
Cream Cheese Frosting, 139
Cream of Broccoli Soup, 32
Cream of Spinach Soup, 32
Creamy Cocoa, 40
Creamy Salmon Tarragon Bake, 98
Crunchy Granola, 124
Crunchy Tuna Casserole, 99
Curried Almonds, 26
Custard Sauce, 107

D

Defrosting, 16
Desserts,
  see also Cakes, Candies, Frostings,
    Pies, Puddings
  Applesauce, 147
  Baked Apples, 147
  Individual Baking Custards, 145
  Nutty Chocolate Bars, 144
  Strawberry Peach Cobbler, 146

Dough Art, 154, 155
Drying Flowers, 156, 157
Duckling, Charts, 82, 83
Duckling with Orange Currant
  Glaze, 84

E

Easy Crab À La King, 97
Easy Paella, 87
Easy Salisbury Steak, 58
Easy Stuffed Beef Rolls, 50
Eggs,
  Bacon and Egg Ring, 105
  Filled French Omelet, 103
  Ham and Egg Scramble, 103
  Poached Eggs, 102
  Quiche Lorraine, 104
  Scrambled Eggs, 102
  Spinach Pie, 104

F

Farina, 124
Filled French Omelet, 103
Fish, Charts, 94
  see also Salmon, Tuna
  Fisherman's Special, 96
  Poached Fish Fillets, 95
  Rolled Fish Fillets and Vegetables, 96
Fisherman's Special, 96
Flowers,
  Drying Flowers, 156, 157
French Lamb Stew, 79
Frostings,
  Chocolate Frosting, 139
  Cream Cheese Frosting, 139
Fudge, 144

G

Garlic Herb Lamb Roast, 76
Garlic Herb Leg of Lamb, 76
Garlic Shrimp, 26
German Chocolate Snack Cake, 137
German Potato Salad, 116
Glazed Carrot Coins, 119
Glazed Rum Cake, 135
Goulash, 56
Graham Cracker Crust, 141
Granola,
  Crunchy Granola, 124
Grasshopper Pie, 141
Greek Lamb Chops, 77
Green Beans Amandine, 118
Green Peppers,
  Stuffed Green Peppers, 57
Grilling, 21
Grits, 124
Ground Beef,
  Chili, 54
  Easy Salisbury Steak, 58
  Goulash, 56
  Hamburger Pie, 59
  Italian Meatballs and Tomato
    Sauce, 71
  Lasagna, 61
  Mini Meatloaf, 59
  Porcupine Meatballs, 58
  Rolled Italian Meatloaf, 60
  Sloppy Joes, 40
  Stuffed Green Peppers, 50
  Stuffed Herb Burgers, 69
  Swedish Meatballs, 56
  Texas Chili, 54

H

Ham,
  Cheese and Mushroom Ham
    Loaf, 70
  Country Ham Casserole, 68
Ham and Apple Ring, 70
Ham and Egg Scramble, 103
Ham and Split Pea Soup, 35
Ham and Vegetable Chowder, 35
Ham, Cheese and Apple
  Sandwiches, 38
Ham Roll-Ups, 29
Ham Steak with Raisin Sauce, 68
Hamburger,
  see Ground Beef
Hamburger Pie, 59
Herb-Basted Turkey Breast, 88
Herbed Lemon Chicken, 88
Herb Garlic Vinegar, 153
Hoppin' John, 123
Hot Buttered Rum, 42
Hot Butterscotch, 42
Hot Fudge Sauce, 109
Hot Mexicali Party Dip, 29
Hot Pasta Salad, 123

I

Individual Baked Custards, 145
Italian Marinated Roast, 48
Italian Meatballs and Tomato Sauce, 71
Italian Vegetables, 28
Italian Zucchini, 119

J

Jams,
  Orange Pineapple Jam, 151
  Peach Jam, 150
  Strawberry Raspberry Jam, 151
Jellies,
  Spiced Grape Jelly, 150

L

Lamb, Charts, 75
  Classic Lamb Curry, 79
  French Lamb Stew, 79
  Garlic Herb Lamb Roast, 76
  Garlic Herb Leg of Lamb, 76
  Greek Lamb Chops, 77
  Lemon Mint Lamb Kabobs, 78
  Persian Lamb, 77
Lasagna, 61
Lemon Custard Sauce, 107
Lemon Mint Lamb Kabobs, 78
Lemon Sage Pork Chops, 66
Lemon Sauce, 107
Liqueurs,
  Cherry Almond Liqueur, 152
  Peach Liqueur, 152

M

Macaroni, Chart, 122
  Hot Pasta Salad, 123
Macaroni and Cheese, 104
Mandarin Shrimp and Peapods, 95
Marinated Sirloin Tip Roast, 48
Meats,
  see also Beef, Lamb, Pork
  How to Determine Internal
    Temperature, 47

Melba Sauce, 109
Mexicali Party Dip, 29
Microwaves, 6
Microwave-Safe Dishes, 7, 8
Mini Meatloaf, 59
Mocha Cocoa, 40
Mornay Sauce, 107
Mulled Cider, 41
Mushrooms,
  Barley Mushroom Casserole, 125
  Sautéed Mushrooms, 24
  Stuffed Mushrooms, 24

N

New England Clam Chowder, 33
Noodles, Chart, 122
  Citrus Noodles, 122
Noodles Alfredo, 122
Nut Bread, 128
Nuts,
  Shelling, 21
Nutty Chocolate Bars, 144

O

Oats, Chart, 124
  Cinnamon Apricot Oatmeal, 124
  Cinnamon Raisin Oatmeal, 124
Old-Fashioned Pot Roast, 49
Onions,
  Stuffed Onions Florentine, 114
Orange Braised Roast, 48
Orange Pineapple Jam, 150
Orange Warm-Up, 43
Oriental Beef and Broccoli, 53
Oriental Pork and Cabbage, 66
Oven Cooking Bags, 9

P

Paper Towels, 9, 17
Pastas, Chart, 122
  see also Macaroni, Noodles,
    Spaghetti
  Hot Pasta Salad, 123
  Lasagna, 61
Peach Jam, 150
Peach Liqueur, 152
Peas, Chart, 113
  Ham and Split Pea Soup, 35
  Hoppin' John, 123
  Split Pea Soup, 35
Pecan Pie, 140
Persian Lamb, 77
Pie Crusts, Chart, 134
  Chocolate Crumb Crust, 141
  Graham Cracker Crust, 141
  Single Pie Crust, 141
Pies,
  Chocolate Cheese Pie, 139
  Coconut Lemon Meringue Pie, 140
  Grashopper Pie, 141
  Hamburger Pie, 59
  Pecan Pie, 140
  Quiche Lorraine, 104
  Spinach Pie, 104
  Walnut Pie, 140
Pineapple Upside-Down Cake, 136
Pizza Subs, 39
Plastic Wrap, 9
Poached Eggs, 102
Poached Fish Fillets, 95
Poppy Seed Coffee Cake, 131

Porcupine Meatballs, 58
Pork, Charts, 63
  see also Bacon, Ham, Sausage
  Apple-Stuffed Pork Chops, 65
  Bacon, 63
  Lemon Sage Pork Chops, 66
  Oriental Pork and Cabbage, 66
  Savory Pork Chops and Rice, 64
  Seasoned Pork Chops, 66
  Southern Barbecued Ribs, 66
  Stuffed Herb Burgers, 69
  Sweet-and-Sour Pork, 67
Pork Loin Roast with Apricot Glaze, 64
Potatoes, Chart, 113
  German Potato Salad, 116
  Twice-Baked Potatoes, 117
Poultry, Charts, 82, 83
  see Chicken, Cornish Hens,
    Duckling, Turkey
Puddings,
  Chocolate Rice Pudding, 145
  Quick Rice Pudding, 145
  Raisin Bread Pudding, 145
Pumpkin Muffins, 130

Q

Quiche Lorraine, 104
Quick Bologna and Sauerkraut, 73
Quick Chicken and Vegetables, 89
Quick Rice Pudding, 145

R

Raisin Bread Pudding, 145
Raisin Nut Bread, 128
Raisins,
  Plumping, 20
Ratatouille, 115
Reheating, 17
Refreshing the Oven, 21
Reuben Deli Melts, 38
Rice, Chart, 122
  Easy Paella, 87
  Hoppin' John, 123
  Savory Pork Chops and Rice, 64
Rolled Fish Fillets with Vegetables, 96
Rolled Italian Meatloaf, 60
Rosemary-Simmered Chicken, 84
Russian Borscht, 34

S

Salmon,
  Creamy Salmon Tarragon Bake, 98
Salmon Steaks with Dill Butter, 98
Sandwiches,
  Cheese and Bacon Hot Dogs, 37
  Ham, Cheese and Apple
    Sandwiches, 38
  Pizza Subs, 39
  Reuben Deli Melts, 38
  Sloppy Joes, 40
  Tuna Melts, 37
Sauces,
  Brandied Cherry Sauce, 109
  Caramel Sauce, 108
  Cheese Sauce, 108
  Custard Sauce, 107
  Hot Fudge Sauce, 109

Lemon Custard Sauce, 107
Lemon Sauce, 107
Melba Sauce, 109
Mornay Sauce, 107
Sweet-and-Sour Sauce, 107
White Sauce, 108
Sausage, Chart, 72
  Cornish Hens with Apple Sausage
    Stuffing, 85
  Italian Meatballs and Tomato
    Sauce, 71
  Quick Bologna and Sauerkraut, 73
  Sausage and Bean Casserole, 69
  Sausage Stew, 73
  Sausage with Sweet-and-Sour
    Cabbage, 73
Sautéed Mushrooms, 118
Savory Bean Bake, 115
Savory Cabbage Rolls, 55
Savory Pork Chops and Rice, 64
Scallops, Charts, 94
  Coquille Newfoundland, 97
Seafood, Charts, 94
  see also Crab, Scallops, Shrimp
Seasoned Pork Chops, 66
Shielding, 8, 12
  Loaf Dish, 128
  Square Baking Dish, 138
Shrimp, Charts, 94
  Easy Paella, 87
  Garlic Shrimp, 26
  How to Peel and Devein, 27
  Mandarin Shrimp and Peapods, 95
  Tangy Shrimp, 26
Shrimp Creole, 99
Single Pie Crust, 141
Sloppy Joes, 40
Soups,
  Chicken Gumbo, 36
  Cream of Broccoli Soup, 32
  Cream of Spinach Soup, 32
  Ham and Split Pea Soup, 35
  Ham and Vegetable Chowder, 35
  New England Clam Chowder, 33
  Russian Borscht, 34
  Split Pea Soup, 35
  Vegetable Beef Soup, 34
Southern Barbecued Ribs, 66
Spaghetti, Chart, 122
  Italian Meatballs and Tomato
    Sauce, 71
Spiced Grape Jelly, 150
Spiced Sweet Potato Bake, 119
Spinach, Chart, 113
  Cream of Spinach Soup, 32
  Stuffed Onions Florentine, 114
  Wilted Spinach Salad, 116
Spinach Pie, 104
Split Pea Soup, 35
Standing, 13
Stews,
  Beef Stew, 54
  Brunswick Stew, 87
  French Lamb Stew, 79
  Sausage Stew, 73
Strawberry Peach Cobbler, 146
Strawberry Raspberry Jam, 151
Stuffed Beef Rolls, 50
Stuffed Green Peppers, 57

Stuffed Herb Burgers, 69
Stuffed Mushrooms, 24
Stuffed Onions Florentine, 114
Swedish Meatballs, 56
Sweet-and-Sour Pork, 67
Sweet-and-Sour Sauce, 107
Sweet Potatoes, Chart, 113
  Spiced Sweet Potato Bake, 119
Swiss Fondue, 105
Swiss Scalloped Corn, 118

T

Tangy Shrimp, 26
Techniques, 12, 13
Texas Chili, 54
Texas-Style Nachos, 29
Tomatoes,
  Baked Herb Tomatoes, 118
Towels,
  Warming, 21
Tuna,
  Crunchy Tuna Casserole, 99
Tuna Melts, 37
Turkey, Charts, 82, 83
  Herb-Basted Turkey Breast, 88
Turkey À La King, 91
Turkey Tetrazzini, 90
Twice-Baked Potatoes, 117

U

Utensils, 7, 8, 15

V

Vanilla Cake, 137
Vegetable Beef Soup, 34
Vegetables, Chart, 113, 114
  see also individual names
  Italian Vegetables, 28
  Ratatouille, 115
Vegetable Beef Soup, 34
Vinegar,
  Herb Garlic Vinegar, 153

W

Walnut Pie, 140
Wax Paper, 9
Welsh Rarebit, 105
Western Chicken, 86
White Sauce, 108
Wieners, Chart, 72
  Cheese and Bacon Hot Dogs, 37
Wilted Spinach Salad, 116

Y

Yams, 113

Z

Zucchini, Chart, 113
  Italian Zucchini, 119

Printed in Korea '84. 8.